M000306365

Frédéric Delavier | Michael Gundill

STRENGTH TRAINING ANATOMY

FOR ATHLETES

HUMAN KINETICS

EXERCISES FOR EVERY SPORT 65

PART III

TRAINING PROGRAMS FOR PARTICULAR SPORTS 159

WHY WRITE THIS BOOK?

There are plenty of books about strength training for athletes. So how is this book different? Simply because most of the other books start from the premise that all athletes have the same anatomy and the same morphology. Though we are all basically made the same, there are huge morphological and anatomical differences from one athlete to another. In this book, instead of showing "all-purpose" anatomy, we highlight the major anatomical differences between individuals. And most importantly, we explain the consequences of these differences, which affect performance, before offering you solutions so that you can customize your own strength training program.

We begin by analyzing the morphological characteristics of elite athletes in their respective sports. Then we show you how to compare your own anatomy to that of elite athletes to study the similarities and differences. The study of these anatomical and morphological variations will give you the following information:

❶ *Athletic movements specific to an athlete's body structure.* Given that each type of motion recruits muscles differently, it is essential to understand how your own morphology influences muscle recruitment. Once you understand the importance of the muscles identified in each of your athletic movements, you must strengthen those muscles using an individualized strength training program.

❷ *Strengths and weaknesses.* Strengthening these weak points is the primary focus of your strength training.

❸ *The risk of injuries.* The risk is not the same for everyone; it differs depending on your anatomy and your movements.

❹ *Differences in susceptibility to injury.* As an example, some people have frequent back pain, while others have fragile knees. Here once again, an individual analysis is required, and your strength training program should be customized to account for your own risk of injury.

STRENGTH TRAINING SHOULD BE EVER PRESENT

Strength training for an athlete is not just for strengthening the body. Some strength training exercises are perfect for warming up prior to strength training, to optimize your strength and endurance while decreasing your risk of injury. For this purpose, do the exercises before your typical warm-up to prepare those very specific, sensitive areas that are so often neglected, such as the rotator muscles in the hips and shoulders. After your workout, once you are home, you should do other strength training exercises to enhance your recovery. The goal is to accelerate the recovery of your muscles, back, tendons, and ligaments so that you can work out again sooner while reducing the risk of injury.

A WIDE VARIETY OF MOVEMENTS

Working out in a gym using professional equipment is important. However, you should understand that a gym workout is just part of the optimal strength training program—strength training exercises also need to be done at home. So that you can get stronger both in the gym and at home, several variations are provided for every exercise. Many warm-up and recovery exercises can be done using a towel or a simple resistance band.

There are three types of strength training: warm-up, strengthening, and recovery. The difference between the three lies in the intensity as well as the volume of work.

PREPARATORY STRENGTH TRAINING

Many athletes play multiple sports at the same time, especially seasonal sports such as skiing or surfing. For these athletes, advance physical preparation is really important; it allows the athlete to begin the season with the best effort right from the start, without being out of shape at the beginning or experiencing injuries during the opening days.

A GUIDE FOR COACHES

This book is also intended for all coaches who train athletes participating in a variety of sports. Quite often, their workouts are inspired by bodybuilding, as are the intensification techniques and even the strength training exercises themselves. As we will show you, even though there are similarities between bodybuilding and athletic strength training, there are many differences that must be taken into consideration.

THE BASIC PRINCIPLES
OF STRENGTH TRAINING
BY SPORT

RUNNING SPORTS

TRAIN YOUR THIGHS SO YOU CAN RUN FASTER

Running is at the heart of many sports. Given its importance, we begin with this question: How can strength training help us run faster? How can strength training improve athletic performance, whether that means power, explosiveness, or endurance?

Strength training allows you not only to gain speed, but also to reduce the risk of injuries that are inherent in many sports. If you are already experiencing pain, the location of the pain can provide important clues about the weak links underlying these injuries. These areas are not strong enough to support the stress your body experiences, and it is on these areas that you need to focus your efforts at recovery and muscle strengthening.

To understand which muscles you should focus on first, begin by studying your personal running style. Contrary to popular belief, all people do not use their muscles in exactly the same way while running. You can see this by observing the shape of your own muscles. We will look at this more closely to help you customize your strength training workouts.

CAN YOU SKIP STRENGTH TRAINING?

First, to get better at running, you have to run. But studies have clearly shown that gaining power in the thighs through strength training translates mechanically into better race times.[1] It is possible to optimize these benefits while minimizing the time you spend strength training if you focus first on the muscles that runners use the most. Among all these muscles, as described in detail later on, you should first work on your weakest muscle groups. For example, if you have trouble lifting your knees with enough power, your strength training program should focus on the hip flexors. If you are not stable when you run, then you must focus on the stabilizing muscles of the hip and pelvis.

What Is the Impact of Strength Training on the Volume of Work?

Should you simply add strength training to your current running program? Or is it better to run a little less so you can spend more time doing strength training? Or, given a set number of hours to train, is it better to practice only running?

Each strategy has advantages and drawbacks. Once athletes have identified all the pros and cons, they should use this information to establish their own personal balance.

■ THE ADVANTAGES OF ADDITION

✪ This is the simplest strategy. This way you do not have to wonder how to scale back, which is not always an easy thing to decide.

✪ An addition is one way to make progress and reach a new level of training volume.

■ THE ADVANTAGES OF MAINTAINING A CONSISTENT VOLUME OF WORK

✪ It is easier to recover.

✪ This is an ideal strategy when you have little time to devote to training.

✪ By running less, you reduce your risk of overuse injuries.

✪ Between sport seasons, it is easier to sacrifice running time, knowing that what you gain through strength training is relatively easy to conserve with one simple strength training session per week thereafter. During competition periods, you can decrease the amount of time you spend strength training and increase the amount of time you spend running.

No matter your choice, we will provide you with the training programs and exercises that are most appropriate for your morphology and your physiological needs. This will allow you to spend less time strength training while obtaining the best possible results.

HOW CAN STRENGTH TRAINING HELP YOU RUN FASTER?

Though it seems obvious that strength training can help you run faster, how exactly does this happen? Strength training provides six broad categories of different, but complementary, benefits.

❶ Strength Training Protects You From Aches and Pains

Muscle soreness takes a lot of time to go away, and it can really interfere with your performance.

When you begin doing strength training, the first thing you will notice is muscle soreness. Then, after a certain number of workouts, the intensity of the soreness will gradually lessen. The muscles start to "immunize" themselves. This immunization against pain begins rapidly, before strength training has caused even the smallest change in your muscles or nerves.[2]

The advantage for athletes is that if their own sport also causes muscle soreness that slows down recovery, strength training will reduce both the rate and the severity of the muscle soreness. This will further accelerate recovery time between two workouts and allow you to train again quickly.[3] This immunization is even more important if you do seasonal sports like skiing or surfing; strength training can be done anywhere and at any time, including in your own home.

② Strength Training Prevents Sports Injuries

The goal of strength training is, above all, to strengthen the body. Athletes who regularly do strength training decrease their rate of injuries by 30 to 50 percent in their respective activities.[4] By comparison, stretching alone has no preventive effect.[4]

You can use various strategies to prevent injuries; we describe these later.

■ SPECIFIC STRENGTHENING FOR VARIOUS WEAK LINKS

At the heart of each muscle is a weak area where the muscle and the tendon meet, called the myotendinous junction. This huge weak area is the one most likely to suffer trauma, or even tears.[6] Studies show that strength training specifically strengthens this area. So if you are someone who experiences hamstring tears easily, a strength-specific training program can be designed to remedy this vulnerability.

▲ Among athletes competing in hurdles, doctors noticed that the stronger the athlete was in the deadlift, the better that athlete could tolerate a larger amount of running without getting hurt. On the other hand, a higher number of injuries was associated with muscle weaknesses.[5]

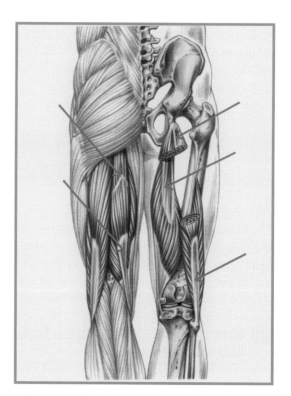

▲ The myotendinous junctions of the hamstrings are numerous and spread out, which explains why these muscles are so prone to tears.

■ RECALIBRATING STRENGTH

Strength training can also be used to correct strength imbalances between the left and right sides of the body.[7] These strength imbalances, which occur frequently, including among high-level athletes, are one risk factor for injury that is easy to correct. Similarly, we will see why it is important to balance strength between antagonistic muscles (quadriceps, hamstrings) since running in itself tends to accentuate these differences. Another asymmetry, which is a cause of decreased performance, is the difference between concentric strength (when the muscle shortens) and eccentric strength (the muscle tone when the muscle lengthens).[8] During a forced stretch—for example, when pitchers pull on their pectoral muscles while moving their arm forward before throwing the ball—the muscles can be injured due to the extreme tension and speed of the movement.

A sedentary person suffers from restricted muscle contraction during the lengthening phase. Strength training removes this restriction, which recalibrates the level of effectiveness between concentric strength and eccentric strength, thereby increasing performance and preventing injury.[9]

■ STRENGTH TRAINING HELPS YOU RUN BETTER

By working the muscles that are not strengthened sufficiently during running, a weekly strength training session over 48 weeks improves running technique in endurance athletes better than running itself.[10] Better positioning of the knees and hips, helped by increased strength, significantly reduces the risk of typical running injuries.[10] Additionally, runners with stronger muscles also find that the classic loss of good running form due to fatigue happens less often.[11]

AN INJURY IS NOT JUST PHYSICAL PAIN

More so than for other people, an athlete who has injury can experience depression.[12] For an athlete, an injury is not just physical pain. Because the injury affects the ability to train, it often causes mental suffering, which can profoundly affect quality of life.

The more serious the injury is, the worse the depression can be.[13] Preventing injuries should therefore be a priority for every athlete.

---

③ Strength Training Increases the Speed of Strength Propagation

During a stride, the foot has very little contact with the ground. So, during this brief amount of time, the transmission of force has to be as powerful as possible. This depends on the rate of force development (RFD) within the muscles. The contact is so brief that the muscle does not have enough time to express its full power; only a certain percentage of its maximum strength can be used. To run faster, you must increase the total force of the muscle and the speed with which force develops within the muscle. This is possible through strength training.

■ UNDERSTANDING RFD

During a sprint, the foot is in contact with the ground for less than a hundredth of a second. This leaves little time, when you consider that, on average, a muscle needs 600 to 900 milliseconds to reach its maximum strength.

In 50 milliseconds, a person who is sedentary can recruit about 15 percent of their strength versus about 26 percent in a well-trained athlete. This is because of a differential in the RFD, which is twice as fast in champion athletes. This quality depends in large part on the nervous system (your genetics), but it can be improved with training, especially with strength training.

If you transmit only 15 percent of your maximum power during a stride, you can make your stride more efficient by increasing your maximum strength. If your maximum strength increases from 50 kilograms to 100 kilograms, your stride will be twice as powerful, even with a poor RFD. The ideal is, of course, to increase both your maximum strength and your RFD at the same time. In beginners, 14 weeks of strength training using heavy weights that allowed them to do just 3 to 10 reps increased the RFD by

✪ 23 percent during a contraction shorter than 50 milliseconds and
✪ 17 percent during the following 100 to 200 milliseconds.

Maximum strength increased by 16 percent.[14]

■ SYNERGY BETWEEN STRENGTH TRAINING AND RUNNING

The key to sprinting and running is contact with the ground, but that contact should be as brief as possible. To achieve this, runners' muscles learn to contract ahead of time, just before the runner touches the ground, which stabilizes the muscle–tendon ensemble. Since the muscle has already started to contract before the foot touches the ground, it can express a greater percentage of its power during actual ground contact. Runners develop this ability through sprint training and plyometrics (for example, jumping lunges) more than with strength training. Still, strength training can increase muscle strength better than actual running, which makes these different types of workouts perfectly complementary.

❹ Strength Training Leads to Proprioceptive Gains

As you work your body regularly through strength training, the brain, via the nervous system, learns to control the muscles better. This is why you move a bit chaotically when you begin strength training but the movements get smoother over time. At the beginning, you might not be able to feel exactly which muscles you are working, but you will feel the muscles better and better as you continue training. This improved control over the muscles is called *proprioception.*

Furthermore, studies have shown that with poor proprioception, your athletic movements will be less effective, and your risk of injury will be higher. The body naturally has trouble determining the exact position of the muscles during movement, and this can place the limbs in positions that are precarious and ineffective and that can lead to injuries. In the same way, the brain has a hard time deciding how much force it should send to the muscles compared to how much they need in a given situation.

Of course, learning a sport improves proprioception, but this improvement will happen even faster if you also do strength training exercises.

You should also know that an injury seriously interferes with proprioception, which explains why muscle and tendon injuries tend to recur.[15] Studies show that a first injury can quickly snowball and actually promote other injuries.[16] For example, a knee injury greatly increases the risk of an injury to the other knee.[17] You can use strength training to break this vicious cycle.

⑤ Strength Training Increases Endurance

On longer-distance runs, there is another factor to consider: the amount of energy expended with each stride. The less energy expended, the farther or faster you can run. This is the fifth factor that can be improved through strength training, and it translates to increased endurance (see Understanding the Concept of Running Economy on the next page).

■ RUNNING ECONOMY

People first learned about the benefits of strength training for distance runners when Paavolainen's 1999 study was published.[18] Until then, people thought that training for endurance and strength simultaneously would cause a lot of problems; endurance training would reduce gains in power, and strength training would decrease the endurance of high-level athletes.

Starting from the principle that after several years of doing only intense endurance training, high-level athletes would reach a plateau, Leena Paavolainen suggested that strength training could push the main physiological limits causing this stagnation in endurance: the inability to improve running economy beyond

a certain point. To test the hypothesis, she worked with high-level endurance runners. For nine weeks in the off-season, some of these runners reduced their running volume by 32 percent so that they could include strength training.[18] After nine weeks, the time required to run 5,000 meters decreased by 3.1 percent in the group that did strength training, but run times tended to get worse in the group that did only running. Strength training improved running economy more than 8 percent.

Depending on the study, gains in running economy range from 2 percent to 8 percent, with these numbers varying based on the type of strength training, duration, and, naturally, the capacity of the athletes to react (or not) to the added work volume represented by strength training sessions.[19] As an example, in high-level runners who compete at distances of 1,500 to 10,000 meters, a strength training program was introduced as two weekly training sessions, each lasting for one hour, for a total of 40 weeks.[20] A second group followed the same running training program but without the strength training so that the two groups could be compared. Thus, the strength training program was in addition to the running training program. The first 20 weeks were in the off-season, and the following 20 weeks took place during the competition season.

Compared to the group who did no strength training, the runners who did strength training saw their running economy improve by 3.5 percent. Furthermore, the benefits of strength training occurred very quickly, with running economy improving by 4.8 percent during the first 20 weeks.

UNDERSTANDING THE CONCEPT OF RUNNING ECONOMY

Just like a car, running consumes fuel. In the case of a car, you can determine how much gas it takes to go 100 miles. Scientists can do the same calculations for athletes. For a given speed and distance, how much energy is used?

Though the $\dot{V}O_2$max represents the main predictive quality of endurance in beginners, this is not the case in higher-level athletes. For them, running economy is what counts. This is the number one factor used to predict performance in a high-level distance runner. The more economical a champion is, the better that person's performance will be.

It is in this critical aspect of endurance that strength training makes the difference compared to the specific training sessions for a particular sport. Strength training makes the muscle and the nervous system more efficient, and this allows the body to conserve fuel. This "savings" allows you to either run faster or run for a longer distance.

By increasing the capacity of the thighs and calves to store more elastic energy and to respond better to each stride, strength training saves energy. In fact, playing with the elasticity of the muscles and tendons does not just allow you to gain speed; it also uses much less energy than a true voluntary contraction. Strength training makes the muscles stiffer and thus better able to rebound from the ground.

This is similar to bouncing a ball: If the ball is soft because it does not have enough air in it, it flattens more on the ground, which increases the contact time and prevents it from bouncing very high. You lose on both sides of this equation. Strength training is like adding air to the ball. Once the ball is fully inflated, it does not flatten as much on the ground, which reduces the contact time with the ground and allows it to bounce higher. By being stiffer at the moment of foot–ground contact, the muscles and tendons of the thighs and calves are better able to bounce back and to save energy, all while decreasing friction during contact.

Thanks to this improved running economy, increased strength (+1 percent), and improved capacity to return elastic energy (+4 percent), the $\dot{V}O_2$max increased by 3.5 percent over the first 20 weeks and by 4 percent over the entire 40 weeks. This improvement did not occur in the group that did only running.

Other mechanisms lead to these energy savings. For example, eight weeks of strength training for the thighs reduced by 16 percent the number of motor units necessary for the muscles to express 70 percent of their maximum force.[21] The result of this savings in muscle fiber recruitment is a substantial gain in endurance. The moral of the story: Adding strength training does not reduce endurance; it increases it.[22]

6 Targeted Recovery Strength Training Helps You to Recover Faster Between Workouts

People often say that as your athletic abilities increase, you need to do less strength training. The reality is much more nuanced. In fact, strength training is not just for increasing muscle strength, power, and endurance; it can also help accelerate the body's recovery after intense athletic activity. Indeed, strength training can activate the process of muscle, tendon, and joint regeneration, thereby promoting recovery.

Seen through the lens of recovery, the better an athlete is, the more that athlete needs to increase the volume of strength training recovery work. But be aware that, as we will show in the last part of this book (see Training Programs for Particular Sports on p. 159), strength training to increase strength or power is very different from strength training that promotes faster recovery. However, the higher your athletic level and the more physical activity you do (as competition season approaches, for example), the more you need to moderate the amount of intense strength training you do.

Conclusion

Strength training allows you to improve muscle qualities in ways that cannot be developed by just practicing a sport. It can improve any kind of performance, whether it is a physical challenge that requires maximum explosive strength over a short period of time, a competition that demands endurance, or any physical activity in between these two extremes that requires a combination of these two physical qualities.[23]

■ LONG-LASTING BENEFITS

Though changes may be slow in the beginning, there are benefits during the competition season, because the effects of strength training last for several weeks, even after weight training has stopped completely. Studies show that gains in strength acquired from six weeks of strength training last for four weeks after training has stopped.[24] Gains in endurance can last for at least five weeks after training stops, when the athlete begins competing again.[22]

Muscle improvements can be durably maintained with just a fraction of the strength training that was necessary to obtain them in the first place. For example, during competition season, a weekly strength training session continues to increase strength by 7 percent, while strength decreases by 8 percent in a group that does no strength training.

HOW FAST SHOULD YOU GO WITH STRENGTH TRAINING?

It is always hard to make predictions. Even though everyone responds differently to the beneficial effects of strength training, once the first aches and pains have resolved, the gains appear relatively quickly. Strength training is a powerful wake-up call to the nerves, even in a champion athlete. Demanding an unusual level of work from the muscles forces the brain to reorganize nerve connections quickly to be able to respond to this new athletic requirement. The protective effect against injury takes longer; it can take several weeks to appear since the body needs to restructure the tissues of the muscles and tendons completely. This remodeling is more fastidious than what happens in the nervous system—and especially since the first few workouts can damage tissues instead of strengthening them. So you should begin slowly, add on gradually, and perhaps even decrease the volume of your sport-specific training for a brief period of time.

WHICH MUSCLES SHOULD YOU FOCUS ON DURING STRENGTH TRAINING?

Start With a Customized Strength Training Program

The goal of individualized strength training as a function of your needs and your weaknesses is the opposite of what is typical. A typical program is the same for everyone and varies only depending on a person's fitness level. To customize your program the best way, you need to understand first what your sport requires from your muscles and your body. Then you need to understand the roles of different muscles, because strength training can affect all three phases of running: lifting the knee, landing on the ground, and propelling the leg backward.

Don't We All Run Using the Same Muscles?

Yes, we all run using the same muscles, but what differs from one athlete to another is the degree to which each muscle is recruited. These variations obviously will have a significant influence on the development of a strength training program, which should be customized to reflect this hierarchy of importance.

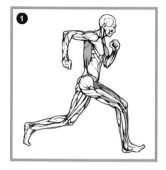

❶ The muscles that contract are shown in red (rectus femoris and tensor fasciae latae); these produce the main effort to propel the right knee up and forward. The muscles that support this movement are shown in orange.

❷ During the same movement, the muscles shown in blue stretch and store up the maximum amount of elastic energy. The muscles in purple do not stretch much, so they store less elastic energy.

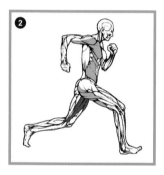

❸ The contraction releases, allowing gravity to push the right foot down.

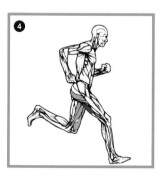

❹ During that movement, the muscles in blue stretch and store the maximum amount of elastic energy. The muscles in purple do not stretch much, so they store less elastic energy.

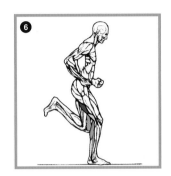

5 The foot touches the ground, causing a strong contraction in the calves, quadriceps, and gluteus medius (muscles in red). The muscles that support this effort are shown in orange.

6 During the same movement, the muscles shown in blue stretch and store the maximum amount of elastic energy. The muscles in purple do not stretch much, so they store less elastic energy.

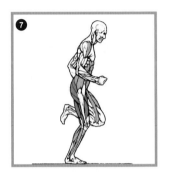

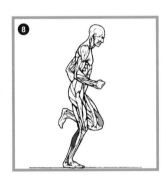

7 The foot moves backward, causing a strong contraction in the quadriceps, hamstrings, and gluteus maximus (muscles in red). The muscles in orange support the work of the muscles in red.

8 During the same movement, the muscles shown in blue stretch and store the maximum amount of elastic energy. The muscles in purple do not stretch much, so they store less elastic energy.

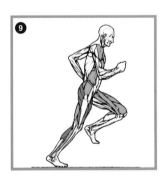

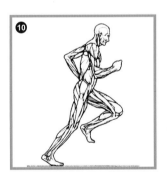

9 The foot is propelled backward through a strong contraction in the calf, quadriceps, and gluteus maximus (muscles in red). The muscles in orange support the effort of the muscles in red.

10 During the same movement, the muscles shown in blue stretch and store the maximum amount of elastic energy.

11 Shown in red, the rectus femoris contracts again; it is responsible for the main effort of propelling the left knee up and forward. The muscles in orange support this movement.

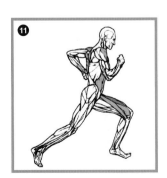

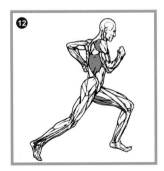

12 During the same movement, the muscles shown in blue stretch and store the maximum amount of elastic energy.

Morphological Analysis of Champion Sprinters' Thighs

Typically, good sprinters have seemingly endless thighs, with long tibias. Paradoxically, their muscles are short because their tendons are lengthened in the calves, quadriceps, adductors, and, to a certain extent, the hamstrings (see the drawing below). The advantage of this configuration is that it provides a really good lever. Long tendons accumulate and release stored elastic energy better with every stride. Short muscles allow the limbs to lengthen, which permits dynamic forward movement. The muscles that drive a sprint, which include the glutes, the tensor fasciae latae, and the iliopsoas, are thus closer to the center of gravity.

Contrast this with longer muscles: The thighs are heavier, and the lever is not well suited for explosive movement. The bigger the calves are, the more they restrict the lever of the knee. This means the movement is mechanically slower. This configuration does permit a more powerful start. But after the first few seconds, the excess muscle weight as well as the lower capacity for storing and releasing elastic energy heralds the beginning of fatigue. The end of the sprint is slower because of the shorter tendons. In contrast, sprinters with longer tendons conserve energy since they run with more of a bounce.

Obviously, many athletes fall somewhere in between the two extremes of a champion with very long tendons (the majority) and a champion with very short tendons (the minority).

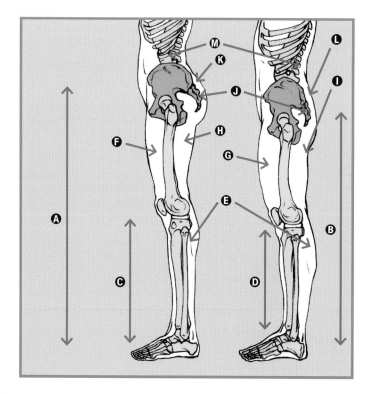

◄ On the left is the typical morphology of running champions. On the right is a morphology that is less advantageous for running.
Ⓐ Never-ending leg
Ⓑ A shorter leg
Ⓒ A long tibia
Ⓓ A shorter tibia
Ⓔ A calf that is all tendons on the left and all muscles on the right
Ⓕ Quadriceps and hamstrings Ⓗ that are more tendinous
Ⓖ Quadriceps and hamstrings Ⓘ that are more muscular
Ⓙ Strong pelvic tilt on the left and weak pelvic tilt on the right
Ⓚ Glutes that stick out more, are rounder, and are more muscular
Ⓛ Glutes that stick out less, are flatter, and are less muscular
Ⓜ Even though the lumbar curve is similar, because of the greater pelvic tilt, the person on the left appears more arched than the person on the right

You must analyze your own body, muscle by muscle, to determine if each of your muscle groups consists more of tendons or muscles, since this distinction has repercussions not only on your running strategy but also on your strength training method.

■ PRACTICAL APPLICATIONS FOR RUNNING

The shorter the locomotor muscles are, because of their long tendons, the more you can lengthen your stride to run fast. In contrast, with long muscles, there is no benefit to lengthening your stride. It is better to adopt a shorter, faster stride because a quicker stride means you do not have to lift up a really heavy thigh.

■ PRACTICAL APPLICATIONS FOR STRENGTH TRAINING

With short muscles, you can do more sets since it is harder to build volume in these more tendinous muscles. You can work in shorter sets and do more of them to improve the explosiveness of your starts. Doing this will not mean that your stride gets heavier. The longer your femur is, the more the focus is on the glutes and the hamstrings, less so on the quadriceps.

With long muscles, especially long and heavy calves, you should do fewer sets to avoid overdeveloping them. The same is true for the thighs. Accentuate the muscles that are very close to the center of gravity (rectus femoris and especially the psoas), which will not make your stride heavier. You can try to run using your glutes more and a little less of your quadriceps. The sets should be a bit longer to increase your strength and endurance and to delay the onset of fatigue at the end of a race.

SPEED ALTERS MUSCLE RECRUITMENT

The speed at which you run also affects your muscle recruitment strategy. For example, scientific measurements show that, on average, compared to a speed of 3.5 meters per second, accelerating to 8.95 meters per second proportionally increases the recruitment of the glutes versus the quadriceps.[25]

The reason is largely a longer stride that stretches the glutes and the hamstrings to a greater degree. You also have to consider your speed when determining the importance of each muscle group for strength training.

Morphological Analysis of the Torso

In running, the role of the arms is not just to help maintain a regular cadence or to provide good balance for the body.[26] The arms also contribute to the body's forward movement, especially in the starting phase. In team sports, the arms play an even more important role: You can use them to protect yourself, push someone away, or block an opponent.

The propulsive force of the arms does not really come from the biceps or the triceps. It mostly comes from the shoulders, chest, and back, not to mention the rotation of the torso and the hips, which help to increase the range of arm movement (see the drawings on pp. 20-21).

A sprinter who is all tendons on the lower part of the body will have more muscles on the upper body. This is especially true in the arms and shoulders, which are naturally made of up of long muscles and short tendons.

The chest area is limited, despite having large shoulders. As for the abdomen, it is long and thin. However, a sprinter who is all muscle on the thighs will have shorter muscles with longer tendons on the torso. This sprinter's abdomen will be larger and stockier.

The Impact of Calf Morphology on the Stride

■ CALVES FULL OF TENDONS VERSUS CALVES FULL OF MUSCLES

In the sprint, you see two main types of calves. Most sprinters have very thin, tendinous calves with small muscles, like Usain Bolt. They can bounce using their calves and use the strength in their hamstrings and glutes for acceleration.

On the other hand, a minority of sprinters, like Kiryu Yoshihide from Japan, have thick, well-muscled calves with short tendons. They use the strength of their calves and quadriceps to run. Given their very different morphologies, these two types of champions should not use the same strength training program for sprinting.

Though a very muscular calf can be advantageous for an explosive start, it can handicap the rest of the race because of its weight and can restrict oxygenation because of its volume. In fact, the larger a muscle fiber is, the harder it is for oxygen from the blood to reach the mitochondria (these are the structures that manufacture ATP, which is the cell's energy source).[27] Though they are harder to lift, which can slow down the stride, thick calves fall more heavily on the ground, and this increases the rebound, especially when the Achilles tendon is stiff.

The smaller the calcaneus is ❶, the more range of motion and flexibility the ankle has; however, this means the lever is also less powerful. You must compensate for this poor lever by adding muscle so that the calves can easily lift the body with each step.

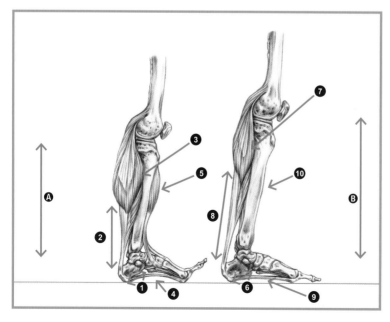

❹ The combination of a short tibia and long muscles is not as well suited for running due to greater muscle mass.

❺ The combination of a long tibia and short muscles allows you to run faster for a longer period of time.

To have the maximum amount of muscle fibers, the tendon must be short ❷, leaving more space for the muscles ❸. The smaller the calcaneus is, the steeper the arch ❹ and the longer and more developed the tibialis anterior (the muscle on the shin) will be ❺. The longer the calcaneus is ❻, the less range of motion and flexibility there is in the ankle, but the more powerful the lever will be. The calf needs less muscle fiber for locomotion ❼, which means it has a longer tendon ❽. The longer the calcaneus is, the flatter the arch ❾ and the shorter and less developed the tibialis anterior will be ❿.

■ THE KEY ROLE OF THE CALF TENDON

After using the strength in the muscles to accelerate, maintaining that speed depends a great deal on an athlete's rebound capacity. Champions who can maintain better speed are those who brake the least when their foot touches the ground, which is, more or less, the least amount of contact possible.[28] At first, this might seem counterintuitive, but research shows that a stiff Achilles tendon, coupled with stiff muscles, allows you to run faster by reducing the time the foot is touching the ground.[29, 30, 31] In other words, the stiffer the tendon is, the more elastic energy allows you to rebound quickly and forcefully from the ground.[32] This is why you run faster on the ground than on sand; however, it is less traumatic to run on sand.

Additionally, medical analyses have shown that the longer the calf tendon is, the more endurance a runner has because of much better running economy.[33, 34] In fact, if we view the calf tendon as a spring, the longer it is, the more effectively it will rebound.[35] Obviously, we cannot alter the length of the tendon; this is genetically programmed. However, strength training can help optimize the rebounding capacity in the calves. Given equal spring (tendon) length, the stiffer the spring is, the more rebound it provides. Strength training can make the tendon stiffer to optimize performance.

The downside of a stiff tendon is that it is injured more often and is more subject to strains—both from missteps and from the accumulation of overuse micro-traumas. Strength training reinforces the structure of the tendon to reduce the chances of injury.

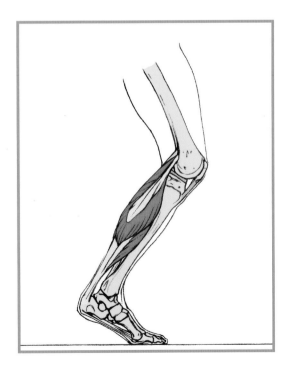

The calf acts like a spring during a race. ▶

The Effects of These Anatomical Differences on Strength Training

Being thought of as an athlete who is not very flexible may seem undesirable, but to us it seems counterproductive to try to gain ankle flexibility at any cost by doing stretching exercises. This is especially true when a long calcaneus and a thin Achilles tendon mean the calf is not naturally suited to being stretched.

Since tendons are much less flexible than muscles, it is normal that a calf made up of tendons is less flexible than a calf made up of muscles. Tendons are naturally less flexible and are not meant to be stretched too much. In contrast, the shorter the calcaneus and the tighter the Achilles tendon, the more naturally supple the calf will be and the more amenable to stretching. Though that is a good thing for sports like cycling, it is much less so for long-distance running. These differences in anatomical properties have important effects on how you do strength training for the calves.

Similarly, in classic leg exercises like squats or leg presses, you should not try to go down too low if your calves are not flexible. Indeed, the only way to compensate for a lack of range of motion in the ankle would be to force more weight on the back (in the squat and the deadlift) and on the knees (in the leg press), which increases the risk of injuries exponentially. There is little point to doing this: It is counterproductive to strive for a maximum range of motion in strength training when the legs are far from reaching their full range of motion during a race. The logic is a bit different when it comes to the hamstrings, because stretching them with strength training exercises makes them stronger, and this protects them from tears.

▲ During a squat, going very deep can be dangerous for the back and the knees in those with long legs that are full of tendons.

▲ Having short legs that are full of muscles makes it easier to go very low during this exercise.

The psoas, the iliacus, and the rectus femoris are three distinct muscles that are interesting to work. Since they are not used very much in daily life, they are naturally weak. On the other hand, since they are close to the center of gravity, they help increase your ability to lift the knees without making your stride heavier. These muscles can help runners with heavy legs speed up their stride. These little improvements are very important for really good sprinters.

The Psoas Muscles

■ MUSCLES OF CHAMPION SPRINTERS
The psoas muscles play a crucial role in locomotion: They help to lift the leg. They are worked intensely during running. Scientific research has shown that the bigger the psoas muscles are, the faster a sprinter can run.[36] In hurdles, the psoas muscle on the side of the thigh that clears the hurdle first is nearly 10 percent bigger than the psoas on the other leg since it must be lifted higher.[37] This means that strengthening the psoas is essential for many sports, especially those that require fast movement.

■ NEGLECTED MUSCLES
The psoas muscles are probably the most neglected muscles in the entire body. Their activity is associated with poor back posture or even with backache. Still, it seems clear that nature did not give us back muscles just so we could experience pain.

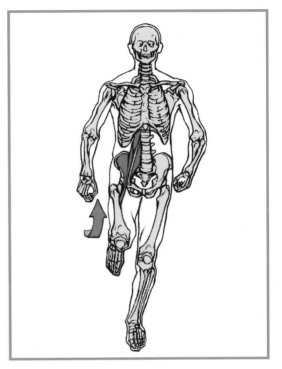

▲ The psoas and the iliac muscles are hidden muscles that you must work to improve how well you can lift your leg.

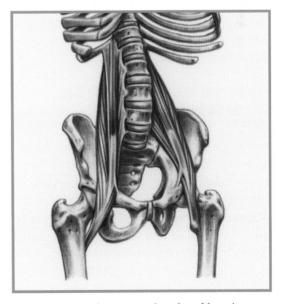

▲ The psoas muscles are near the edge of the spine.

The psoas muscles actually have a protective function. However, in the case of a strength imbalance, too much stiffness, or, in contrast, because of too little muscle tone, their mechanical properties can turn against us.

When the psoas muscles do not contract strongly, they stabilize the lower spine from side to side.[38, 39, 40] If you lift just one leg, say the right one, the right psoas muscle helps to lift the leg while the left psoas also contracts, but only to stabilize the lumbar spine. You can see this dual contraction of the psoas muscles when you walk or run. Sports in which the legs move randomly, like tennis or soccer, tend to cause strength imbalances in the psoas muscles.[41]

A strength imbalance in the psoas muscles can play a part in backaches in athletes, because if the work of lateral stabilization is not equally shared between the right and left sides, then the spine will be unstable with every step. Over time, this can create problems when you are playing sports that require constant movement. Beyond developing them through strength training, you must ensure that the strength in the right and left psoas muscles is as close to equal as possible.

The Rectus Femoris, a Muscle That Should Be Rediscovered

Working synergistically with the psoas and the iliacus, the rectus femoris is a very important muscle for running since it lifts the knee. There are many muscles that propel the knee backward, while there are few that move the thigh forward. The more powerful the thigh is, the faster the stride can be and the more elastic rebound energy it will store.

A lack of strength in the rectus femoris and in the psoas explains why when you want to accelerate your stride past a certain speed and lift the leg higher, you are unable to do it.

■ A FRAGILE MUSCLE
The rectus femoris is a muscle that can tear easily in athletes, especially in the case of a sudden, quick start. Once the foot touches the ground and the leg moves backward, there is a strong eccentric contraction that stretches the muscle. This is the moment when tears are most likely to occur. These tears can be partial tears, but they are generally nearly complete tears.

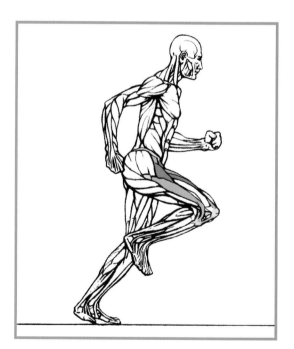

▲ The rectus femoris works together with the psoas and the iliacus to lift the leg.

A tear in the rectus femoris will not stop you from running since the psoas can pick up the slack, but it will seriously slow you down. Additionally, muscle recruitment will become very asymmetric, which can cause problems in other areas like the hips, knees, and ankles. Just as with the hamstrings, you need to strengthen this muscle so that it can more easily handle stretching and releasing energy.

Strength in the rectus femoris is even more important if you have heavy, very muscular thighs with large calves or a long femur or tibia, as opposed to thin thighs and calves that are lighter and much easier to move.

Athletes with muscular calves will need to do dynamic work for the rectus femoris and psoas muscles when they are doing more distance running.

■ A MUSCLE THAT IS NOT OFTEN RECRUITED DURING STRENGTH TRAINING

Among the four muscle heads that make up the quadriceps, the rectus femoris is the only polyarticular muscle (it attaches to both the tibia and the pelvis, which means it covers two joints).

The other three heads of the quadriceps are monoarticular, so they affect only a single joint: the knee. Since they do not attach to the pelvis, they cannot lift the thigh. Truth be told, they weigh it down, slowing down the stride and expending more energy.

Paradoxically, the rectus femoris is the head that is recruited the least during basic strength training exercises for the thighs. The problem is that, in a squat or a leg press, the closer the torso comes to the thighs during the stretching phase of

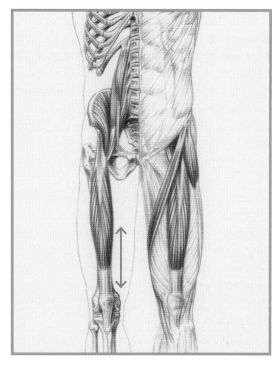

▲ The arrow indicates a fragile zone in the rectus femoris that is susceptible to tears during sports.

the movement, the less the rectus femoris is recruited. As an example, squats recruit the rectus femoris 34 percent less than a leg extension.[42] However, the leg extension is not an ideal exercise for a runner. We will explain why bent-knee leg lifts are much better suited for runners' knees; they recruit the rectus femoris and the psoas simultaneously, which better matches the muscle mobilization required during a stride.

The rectus femoris is also very important for athletes who must run backward during ball or racquet sports, for example.

Bodybuilders who want to work their abs are told not to use their thighs too much when performing those exercises, and the inverse is true for athletes who want to improve their running performance. In fact, by pulling forcefully with the feet and not just the torso during abdominal exercises, you can effectively gain power in the rectus femoris and the psoas. This variation is also beneficial in strength training for cyclists, athletes who participate in combat sports, and even athletes whose sport involves throwing.

▲ The rectus femoris is the only head of the quadriceps that can lift the knee, allowing you to lift the leg while running.

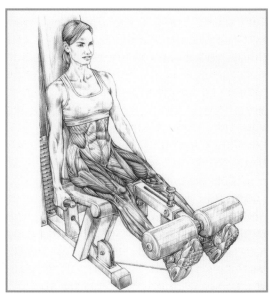

▲ The leg extension recruits the rectus femoris better than the squat or the deadlift.

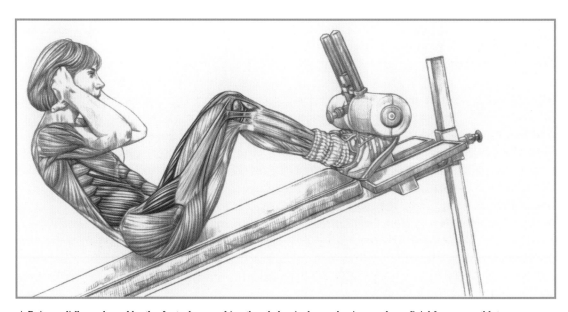

▲ Being solidly anchored by the feet when working the abdominal muscles is very beneficial for many athletes.

In runners, 80 percent of injuries are overuse injuries. Once you have experienced an injury, the risk of a recurrence is very high. But trying to prevent injury through strength training should not work the same muscles and should instead be based on your anatomy. There are similarities and differences between you and other athletes that you must recognize if you want to achieve maximum effectiveness.

Differences in the structure of muscle recruitment that we have just described also affect the risk of injury. The more you run with your hamstrings, the greater the risk of experiencing a muscle tear on the back of your thigh. In contrast, the more you run with your calves, the greater the risk of experiencing chronic exertional compartment syndrome; however, this rarely affects calves with a lot of tendons. The risk of an injury to the Achilles tendon is of course very common.

The Risk of Hamstring Tears Is Not the Same for Everyone

Athletes who have a hip bone that is tilted far backward can more easily place their hamstrings under tension when running. It is much easier for them to recruit the muscles of the back of their thighs because of this better hamstring stretch the moment they bring the leg forward or bend their torso forward. This better stretch and recruitment provides enormous power during a sprint when bringing the leg backward. However, pulling on the hamstring muscles can also cause tears. This is a classic runners' injury.

With a hip bone that is not tilted backward, there is less tension in the hamstrings, reducing their recruitment and the risk of tears in the upper hamstring since, in this case, the runner uses the quadriceps more.

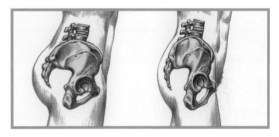

▲ On the left, the hips are tilted forward, which gives the impression that the low back is arched even though this is not the case. On the right, the hips are not very tilted, which reduces the recruitment of the hamstrings during running.

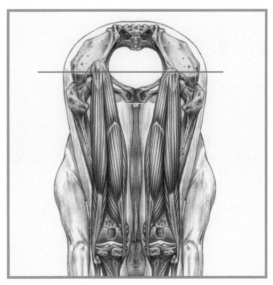

▲ On the left, the higher hip promotes stretching and, thus, recruitment of the hamstrings. On the right side, the hip is not as high, which reduces the risk of hamstring tears.

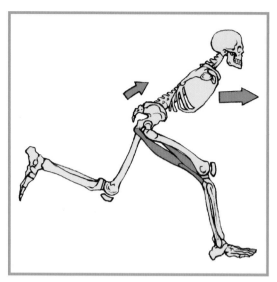

▲ With every stride, the hamstrings are subjected to intense pressure.

No matter what, a lack of strength in the back of the thighs is a weak link during a race, and it increases the risk of hamstring tears and knee pain.

Flexibility Means Nothing Without Strength

It is common practice to recommend stretching to avoid injuries. However, studies are less definitive as to the ability of stretching to prevent injury. Some studies show a benefit, while others show no effect. More and more research, though, shows that stretching can increase the risk of injury.

Concretely, scientific studies showed that six weeks of training, based exclusively on stretching, had no benefit in terms of protecting muscle integrity. When the level of trauma to the hamstrings caused by very intense contractions was compared before and after the six weeks, it was similar, whether or not people did regular stretching exercises.[43]

Indeed, flexibility is nothing without strength. Even though it might seem wonderful to have a large range of motion, if the muscles and tendons are not strengthened ahead of time through appropriate strength training exercises, they will still be fragile in a lengthened position and could easily tear during regular practice for your sport. Of course it is helpful to have a good range of motion, but you must also have prepared your tendons and muscles to withstand strong tension in extreme positions. To respond to these two requirements, in the second part of this book you will find strength training exercises that provide an intense stretch for the hamstrings.

Furthermore, to strengthen the hamstrings in all the positions in which an athlete might need to lengthen them during a particular sport, different variations are provided. In fact, since the hamstrings are essentially polyarticular muscles, they can be stretched from one or both ends at the same time, which provides three distinct types of stretches:

❶ Stretch only from the hips.
❷ Stretch only from the knees.
❸ Simultaneous stretch from the hips and the knees.

Categorizing the stretches this way highlights the two major locations for hamstring tears: high (where they attach to the hips) and low (near the biceps femoris).

Every athlete should focus first on strengthening the weakest area through specific exercises.

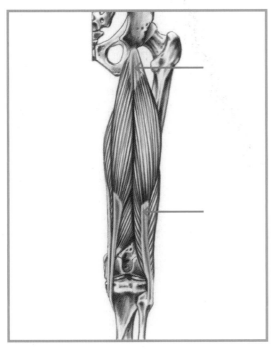

▲ In athletes, the hamstrings generally tear either at the very top or at the bottom.

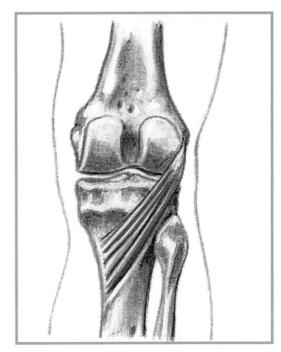

▲ The popliteus muscle.

All Hamstring Exercises Are Not Created Equal!

So that hamstring exercises can be useful and appropriate, you must consider which part of your hamstrings is the most fragile and the most at risk during your sport. Exercises done with bent knees strengthen the biceps femoris,[44] while those that are done while bending the torso target the upper part of the hamstrings.

Hamstring exercises also develop the popliteus muscle, which is located behind the knee and acts as a stabilizer to protect the joint. So it is heavily recruited during running and can become very painful due to the dense nerve network located right next to it.

The Importance of Eccentric Strength for Performance and Preventing Injury

In strength training, weighted eccentric movement is especially important. It allows you better control over the tension experienced when you slow down during the storage and release of energy that happen with every stride for runners or with every jump for jumpers.[45] Eccentric strength training work modifies the direction of muscle fibers slightly, and the fibers become both more effective during running and more resistant to injury.[46, 47]

Negative exercises do not have to be dynamic, which would be dangerous, especially for a beginner. Research shows that even doing eccentric strength training exercises slowly is effective for increasing a runner's speed during a sprint.[48]

Why Focus on the Hamstrings Over the Quadriceps?

There are three reasons why it is easy to tear the hamstrings when you run:

❶ This muscle group has the widest myotendinous junction. Its large size can promote microtears. At first, these may not cause any problems, but as they accumulate, they can cause true, disabling tears.

❷ The relationship between the strength in the quadriceps, which are favored during training, and strength in the hamstrings, which are too often neglected, is very imbalanced.

❸ Running recruits the hamstrings more than the quadriceps; therefore, the muscles on the back of the thigh fatigue more quickly than those on the front of the thigh. This makes them more fragile in terms of tearing.[49, 50] As muscle imbalances in the thigh grow worse, the knee also becomes vulnerable to injury.

Understanding Who Is at Risk for Chronic Exertional Compartment Syndrome

Chronic exertional compartment syndrome (pain affecting the front of the lower leg) primarily affects people with a tibialis anterior muscle that is long and very developed. Because of the tension it creates, it can become easily congested, which cuts off oxygen, compresses the nerves, or can cause necrosis of the blood vessels.

When the tibialis anterior muscle is long and has a short tendon, a runner is more likely to experience chronic exertional compartment syndrome. However, a runner who has flat feet (for nonpathologic reasons, because of a long tendon and a tibialis anterior muscle that is not toned) has little risk of developing this debilitating, painful condition.

MISTAKEN IDEAS ABOUT STRENGTH TRAINING FOR RUNNERS

Many people think that exercises like the squat or the leg press help you run faster because they strengthen the quadriceps. However, though the quadriceps muscles move the leg forward, other muscles, like the hamstrings and glutes, are at least as important during running. The reason these exercises help is because they also recruit the glutes and the hamstrings. Unlike bodybuilders, who are using these exercises to isolate the work to the quadriceps, an athlete tries to work the entire leg, especially the back of the leg and the glutes.

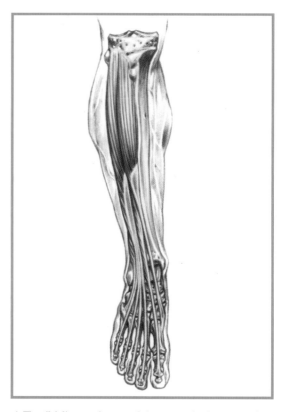

▲ The tibialis anterior muscle's propensity for congestion is even greater the longer and more developed the muscle is.

■ IS SPECIFIC STRENGTH TRAINING A GOOD IDEA?

The bigger the tibialis anterior is and the less supple the fascia is, the greater the risk of pain. The effects of strength training on the tibialis anterior can be a double-edged sword. If the muscle is painful because of repeated trauma due to a structural weakness, then making it stronger though specific exercises can be a very good thing.

However, in the case of chronic exertional compartment syndrome, by making the tibialis anterior bigger, strength training can create more problems than it solves. Then you are faced with a dilemma: How can you optimize the benefits of strength training while minimizing the risk of aggravating the condition?

■ AN ANSWER IN FOUR PARTS

❶ When the foot strikes the ground, the tibialis anterior absorbs the shock, and this creates trauma. So you need to increase its capacity to resist this trauma rather than increasing its pure strength. To do this, favor a training program based on negative reps (by stopping a weight that is stretching the muscle) rather than positive reps (the phase in which you lift the weight by shortening the muscle).

❷ To avoid congestion, do not follow the common practice of doing continuous reps. Ideally, do one rep with the right foot, allowing the left foot to rest. When the right rep is done, repeat on the left foot, allowing the right foot to rest. The goal of this brief rest period between reps is to allow for good blood circulation, which limits the accumulation of blood in the muscle (congestion). Negative reps cause much less congestion compared with positive reps; this is an advantage.

❸ Do not go all out until your muscles cannot move any more. Stop two or three reps before you reach total fatigue or as soon as you feel the slightest congestion.

❹ Work to make the fascia more supple or at least to help its multiple layers of collagen slide more easily against each other. A combination of stretches and massages on a foam roller will work for this.

SEE ALSO

The rotator muscles in the hips and adductors are of the highest importance for runners. They are even more crucial when you are not running exclusively in a straight line, as is the case in ball sports. This subject is covered in the chapter Team Ball Sports (see p. 36).

Strength training for the upper body, which becomes more important as you strive harder for those few hundredths of a second, is discussed in the chapters Swimming and Nautical Sports (see p. 50) and Cycling and Road Sports (see p. 57).

TEAM BALL SPORTS

All the concerns of runners described earlier are identical in ball sports. We will not discuss them again. The primary difference between classic runners and athletes who play on a team is that team athletes do not run forward in a straight line. They also move to the side and must often stop abruptly and then change direction. Their hips are also subjected to enormous stress. It is important to protect the hips by warming them up sufficiently before each workout and by strengthening them. We will also cover here how to prevent knee injuries, especially those injuries that affect the cruciate ligaments.

HIP WORK

Conditioning the Glutes, Abductors, and Hip Rotators Well

The musculature of the hips and glutes tends to make people smile since these muscles are considered essentially feminine and the exercises that work them are not thought of as very masculine. However, beyond these prejudices, if your athletic activity requires running, jumping, or walking, you need to strengthen your glutes, abductors, and hip rotators to perform better and prevent injuries to your lower limbs.

Is it helpful to mention that men and women both have the same muscles? If you have glutes, abductors, and hip rotator muscles, then it is not a question of aesthetics. These muscles fulfill vital functions for locomotion and are indispensable in all sports that use the thighs.

In addition to the increased strength and stability they provide, they are also essential for protection from certain injuries, especially those affecting the hips, knees, and ankles.

The Four Interconnected Functions of the Hip Muscles

These muscles fulfill four essential functions for an athlete:

❶ They allow you to extend the hips backward by using the glutes, including the gluteus maximus, gluteus medius, and gluteus minimus.

❷ They allow you to abduct (spread the legs apart) using the gluteus medius and gluteus minimus as well as the tensor fasciae latae. They also serve as internal rotator muscles and help you pass the ball with the outside of the foot, for example.

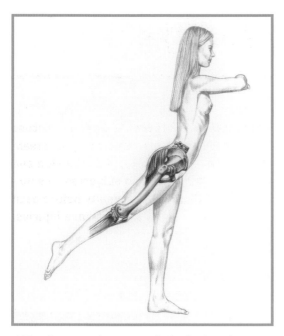

▲ The gluteus maximus moves the leg backward.

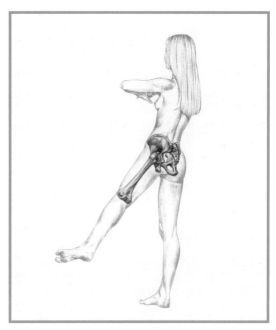

▲ Deep muscle that abducts the leg.

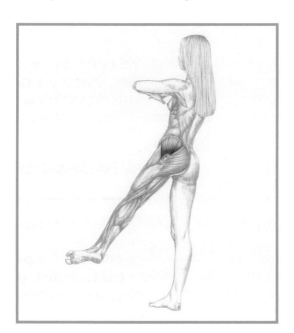

▲ Superficial muscle that abducts the leg.

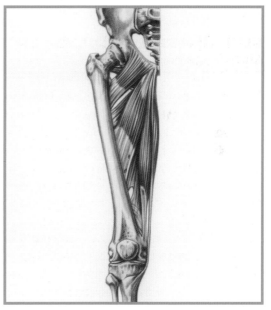

▲ Adductor muscles seen from the front.

❸ They allow you to adduct (bring the legs together) using the adductors and the sartorius. They also help you pass the ball or strike with the inside of the foot.

❹ They allow you to rotate the femur (using the rotator muscles), which means moving the foot from left to right and right to left. For runners, the rotator muscles help stabilize the leg and maintain balance so you can run upright without falling.[1] They also prevent the knees and ankles from ending up in dangerous positions.

These different functions are basically theoretical, because, in reality, the activities of these muscles are not so distinct and separate. In fact, all of these muscles work together as soon you move the leg.

The Rotator Cuff and the Rotator Cuff of the Thighs

More and more athletes understand the purpose of the rotator cuff muscles of the shoulders: They are essential for stabilizing the deltoids, and this increases performance and helps prevent injuries (see Swimming and Nautical Sports on p. 50). The hip rotators and the adductors-abductors do exactly the same thing for the legs. Any weakness on their part or premature fatigue translates into instability and fragility in the hips, knees, and ankles.

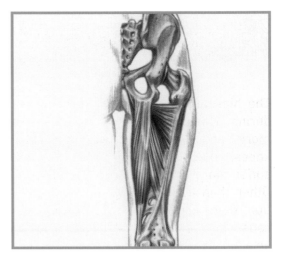

▲ Adductor muscles seen from behind.

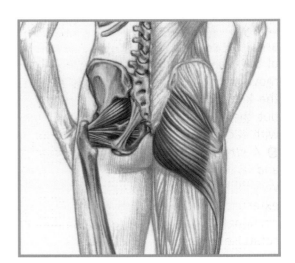

▲ Deep hip rotators (on the left).

CLASSIC HIP PROBLEMS

The hips are subject to a lot of stress during running. Though athletes are more likely to feel these effects in their knees, these same athletes actually suffer more often from hip problems.[2, 3] Other than a morphological predisposition, there are five potentially avoidable causes at the root of these hip issues in an athlete[4]:

❶ *Insufficient warm-up.* The athlete neglects to do a good, specific warm-up.

❷ *Lack of strength.* The longer the femurs are, the stronger the rotator muscles of the hip have to be to avoid the sliding movements that commonly happen with the knees when you land after jumping, but that can also happen imperceptibly with each stride.

❸ *A strength imbalance between agonist and antagonist muscles.* Medical tests very often show an imbalance between external rotator muscles, which are proportionally stronger, and the internal rotator muscles.[5]

❹ *An imbalance between the abductor muscles, which are proportionally stronger, and the adductor muscles.* This happens in many athletes.[6] This does not mean that the abductor muscles are super powerful, because studies also show serious weaknesses there. Rather, it means that the abductors are generally weak and the adductors even more so.[7] This setup also predisposes people to groin injuries.[6, 8, 9]

❺ *A strength imbalance between the right and left thighs.* When there is a large difference between the strength of the muscles on the right side and those on the left side, this difference creates uneven stability between the two legs, exposing athletes to potential injuries.[10]

How Are the Hip Rotator Muscles Involved in Knee Pain?

Knees that crack or that hurt during kneeling are often caused, at least in part, by weak abductor muscles.[11] Studies have shown that, in people who have knee pain, strengthening the abductors through strength training provides rapid relief.[12] Furthermore, strengthening the abductors is more effective for alleviating knee pain than working on the quadriceps.[13] Weakness in the glutes also means there is less stability in the knees.[14]

In a group of women, a four-week program of strength training for the glutes, hamstrings, and abductors caused a reduction in the tension recorded in the knee when landing after jumping.[15] A better muscular cushion greatly reduces the risk of knee injuries.

> ⚠ **Warning!**
>
> Having one leg that is shorter than the other also predisposes you to hip problems. Athletes with this condition must compensate for the difference by using orthotic shoe inserts.

The Role of the Hip Rotator Muscles in Cruciate Ligament Tears

A primary cause of cruciate ligament tears in the knee during a sudden change of direction while running is a lack of strength—not in the quadriceps, but in the hips. In fact, the abnormal movement that causes abnormal torsion in the knee does not happen in the knee, but in the hips when the foot is planted on the ground.

The more the knees tend to turn toward each other when landing after a jump and during running, for example, the more you risk damaging ligaments, both in the knees and in the hips. Female athletes are especially at risk compared to male athletes because women's femurs are more angled than men's.

The Role of the Hip Rotator Muscles in Ankle Problems

Research has also shown that muscle weakness in the hips, especially in the abductors, can lead to ankle injuries.[16, 17]

Preventing Groin Injuries

Erratic running can lead to groin injuries. These types of movements are extremely common in soccer, where athletes are running constantly. When kicking the ball, the athlete increases the risk by causing microtraumas in the adductor muscles, which lead to groin pain.[18, 19] Specific work for the abdominal muscles can be helpful because weaknesses in the lower abdominal muscles also play a role in groin injuries (see Exercises for Combat Sports on p. 144).

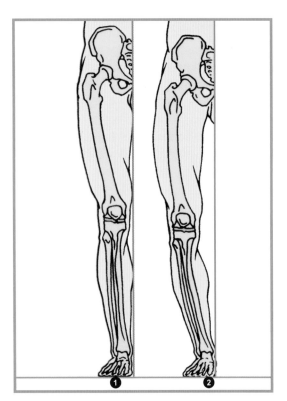

❶ Women's femurs have a marked angle between the hip and the knee. ❷ Men's femurs have a much less marked angle. These morphological differences explain, in part, why female athletes tend to hurt their knees more easily while male athletes tend to hurt their hips more easily.

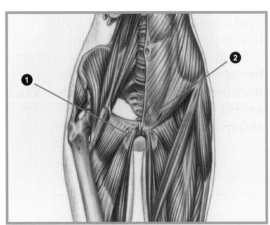

❶ Groin injury affecting the adductors ❷ Parietal abdominal groin injury.

Conclusion

All athletes can benefit from strengthening their hip muscles. You can do this first as a warm-up so that you are not working these muscles while they are cold; this will prevent injuries and optimize performance.

Specific strength training for the adductors, abductors, and hips reduces the severity of hip injuries in professional rugby players by half.[20] Strength training is twice as effective when it specifically targets an individual's weakest muscles as opposed to a generic program that treats all muscles as having equal importance.[20] Thus, it is essential to examine the nature of the pain—since pain varies from one person to another—to try to specifically prevent it through strength training. For example, in male soccer players, groin injuries and hamstring tears are the most frequent injuries, while in female soccer players, quadriceps and cruciate ligament tears predominate.[21]

HOW DO THE HAMSTRINGS PROTECT THE CRUCIATE LIGAMENTS?

Weak hamstrings are associated with a greater incidence of knee injuries.[22] In fact, the quadriceps and the hamstrings compete during running. With weak hip extensors, the torso pulls back and the quadriceps work harder to compensate. The knees, and their ligaments, then must work harder as well. In contrast, when the hip extensors are strong, the torso can tilt forward more. The quadriceps are not asked to work as hard, and this spares the knee joint.

Studies in athletes also show that their hamstrings tend to fatigue more quickly than their quadriceps, and this gradually erodes the protective action of the hamstrings on the knee during sprints.

Movement of the tibia too far forward is another cause of cruciate ligament tears. A lack of strength in the hamstrings means they cannot prevent the tibia from moving forward when the foot is planted on the ground during an abrupt stop, for example.

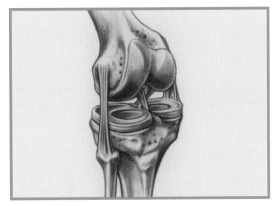

▲ These are the famous cruciate ligaments, which have ended many athletes' careers when torn.

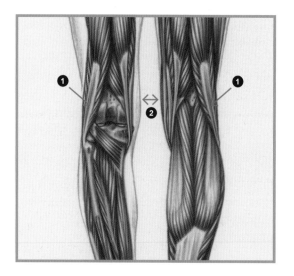

◄ The lower part of the hamstrings helps protect the knees. The biceps femoris ❶ and the semimembranosus ❷ are agonists and protectors of the cruciate ligaments. The biceps femoris turns the foot to the outside and the semimembranosus turns the foot to the inside. While running, when muscles ❶ and ❷ contract isometrically, this guarantees that the feet stay firmly in line. If one of these two muscles or both become fatigued, the feet can no longer stay in line, and this will cause injuries to the knees and ankles. Before any physical activity, you should specifically warm up the lower part of the hamstrings with the hip rotator warm-up exercise (see p. 93), but sitting down, with your calves at a 90-degree angle to the thighs. If your hamstrings are weak or lack endurance, you need to strengthen them using specific hamstring strengthening exercises.

SEE ALSO

Athletes who use their arms to grab or push an opponent away are invited to read the Combat Sports chapter (see p. 61). Those who use their arms to hit or throw a ball will find more details in the chapter Racquet and Throwing Sports (see p. 54). Lastly, you will find strength training exercises for the hamstrings in the chapter Exercises for Running Sports (see p. 66).

GOLF AND SPORTS INVOLVING ROTATION

The rotation of the torso compared to the legs happens to varying degrees in almost all sports. It is especially pronounced in golf, though all athletes really should work both sets of muscles that support the abdomen and protect the lumbar spine.

Statistics show that the power of the drive has increased considerably since the 2000s. And, transferring maximum power to the club implies that you have explosive power. But with any acceleration also comes a braking. The more powerful the swing, the more muscle power you need to stop it without dislocating joints and causing injuries.

Another problem that is common to golf, but is also found in numerous other activities, is pain affecting the inside of the forearms and the wrists. One of the primary goals of strength training for rotation sports is to protect the integrity of the body, especially the back, hips, shoulders, and forearms. Additionally, a good warm-up is even more important if it is for a sport that attracts a lot of older people; statistics show that the incidence of injury in golfers triples after age 54.[1]

PROBLEMS WITH ROTATION

Rotation or Antirotation?

Torso rotation movements are present in a number of sports. This means you must use specific exercises to strengthen the muscles that control this rotation; these are the obliques as well as the lats and the lumbar muscles.

There are two schools of thought concerning strength training via exercises for rotation of the torso to the side. Traditionally, many strengthening exercises involve twisting the torso, and this increases the strength of the torso rotator muscles (see Exercises for Golf and Sports Involving Rotation on p. 100).

▲ The twisting of the body creates increased power in boxing and in all throwing sports, golf, swimming, or running.

However, a new way is emerging. While underscoring the importance of torso rotations and the necessity for working the muscles responsible for rotation, this new method highlights the dangers of these rotation exercises, especially when they are done with weights to make the exercise harder.

Rotation exercises, especially those done with resistance, have no equal when it comes to exacerbating existing injuries. And people can get carried away by the inertia of the weight, which increases the natural range of rotation in the spine.

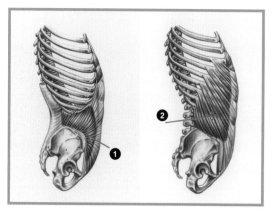

▲ Responsible for rotating the torso, the obliques (internal ❶ and external ❷) play a central role in almost all sports.

Why Antirotation?

This new approach, which is more conservative, advocates static exercises in which you simply have to resist rotation without moving. These are isometric contractions, which have a lot in common with core strength exercises. In antirotation, the exercises are the same as those done dynamically, but you strive not to let the weight pull you. The advantage of antirotation exercises is that you can work the muscles even when an existing injury is exacerbated by the slightest movement of the torso. The disadvantage is that they stimulate the muscles only isometrically, and this does not correspond to the demands of an athletic sport, for example, performing a golf swing.

Nevertheless, a beginner can start to gain muscle using antirotation exercises. Any muscle strengthening always provides numerous benefits, including rotations done by someone who has never done any strength training, especially seniors. The beginner can progress by doing light rotations, and, little by little, gain a larger range of motion over time.

BACK PAIN: THE GOLFER'S PARADOX

Golf places the back in a biomechanically precarious, rotated position. Additionally, it does so in an explosive, violent manner without really strengthening the back muscles. In this context, strength training is clearly appropriate, offering benefits to golfers that their athletic activity alone cannot provide. The protective effect of strength training comes in four forms:

❶ Strength training is an adequate warm-up for the muscles, tendons, ligaments, and joints before golf. Studies have shown that the more time a golfer spends warming up, the lower the chance of injury.[2] But you need to know how to warm up as efficiently as possible.

❷ Strength training helps resolve muscle imbalances between the right and left sides as well as between antagonist muscles, especially in the back, which are inherent in sports that require asymmetrical movement. In this way, it increases stability and reestablishes the main structural balance in the body; this helps protect against injuries in the short and long term.

❸ Focused strength training not only acts to prevent injuries; it will also work the muscles responsible for torso rotation and core support. This will increase the power of your swing.

❹ Strength training can relax and systematically decompress the back after a workout. To do this, hang for a few dozen seconds from a bar. Alternatively, facing a bench or a chair or the edge of a table, lean forward, supporting yourself using your hands. Strive to relax your muscles with the goal of regaining those millimeters lost by the intervertebral discs because of the weight. This will give your back some relief.

▲ You should decompress your back after every workout.

The entire abdominal and lumbar region is interconnected, not only by the muscles, but also by the aponeuroses and the fascia of the muscles in that area.[3] So tension applied to one muscle in the area is transmitted to the entire region. The primary role of the muscles in this zone is to absorb tension, rigidify the abdomen, and protect the lumbar spine.[4] We refer here to core muscles. These muscles help maintain the back in a straight position while it is being subjected to a force that is trying to bend it, either to the side or backward.

Core exercises are effective for strengthening the muscles that stabilize the lower back. But, once you master the basic exercises, the main way to make them more difficult is just to hold them for longer and longer. For example, instead of holding a plank for 30 seconds, hold it for 1 minute, and then 2 or 3.

This strategy is appropriate for endurance athletes like long-distance runners and cyclists, but also for athletes who use their bodies for brief efforts that are very violent. Think of a golfer's swing, a boxer's punch, or a pitcher's throw. Pitchers need lumbar support muscles that react to a quarter turn and that are capable of displaying enormous power in a very limited period of time.

When you do the plank for 1 minute instead of 30 seconds, you have mostly gained endurance and a little strength, but clearly less explosive power. To increase the effectiveness of the plank, we recommend that you combine it with rotation exercises. When you have done your rotation exercise, follow it up immediately with a core exercise; this will be harder to do since the muscles will already be worn out. In the same way, if you work on your abdominal muscles, instead of stopping the set after sit-ups, for example, immediately follow with a plank.

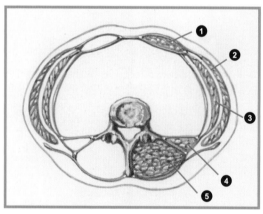

▲ Our muscles form a protective sheath that encircles and protects the lower back:
❶ Rectus abdominis
❷ External oblique
❸ Internal oblique
❹ Quadratus lumborum
❺ Erector spinae

HOW TO STABILIZE THE SHOULDERS EFFECTIVELY

Shoulder pain is often linked to weak supraspinatus muscles.[5] So your objective is to thoroughly warm up all of the rotator cuff muscles that encircle and stabilize the shoulders, especially during large, abrupt movements like a golf swing. Strengthening these stabilizing muscles reduces the risk of shoulder impingement syndrome (see Swimming and Nautical Sports on p. 50). It is imperative to warm up well and strengthen both shoulders, because it is often the nondominant shoulder that you use first.[5]

The backs of the shoulders, working synergistically with the lower-trapezius muscles, not only stabilize the shoulders, but also help give power and precision to your golf swing. In fact, the more stable the shoulders are, the more precise the golf swing. Deltoids poorly supported by stabilizer muscles that are too weak have a tendency to "twist." This makes it difficult to control the shoulders' movement, preventing them from following the torso's rotation precisely. As a result the arms and the club deviate from the proper trajectory.

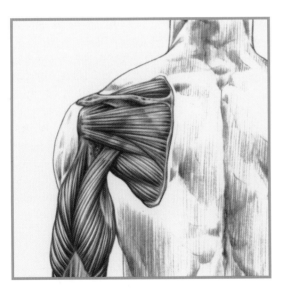

▲ The shoulder rotator muscles stabilize the shoulder, reducing the rate of injuries.

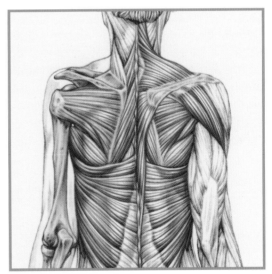

▲ The muscles that surround the shoulder blades also protect against shoulder injuries.

As the name implies, golf elbow (pain on the inside of the forearm) mainly affects golfers, but it can affect all athletes who use their hands a lot, such as surfers, pitchers, or even tennis players. Ideally, you should not wait until you have pain to start worrying about this area since it is so vulnerable to overuse injuries and pain.

Unfortunately, many athletes think that a little ache will eventually go away, and sometimes that does happen. They do not really worry about it until, one day, they are in so much pain that they can no longer use their hands. At that moment, they resolve to do something about the pain. Minor pain, even fleeting, should always be considered an alarm signal from the body. Certainly, it is never too late to act, but it is pointless to wait until the last possible moment, because the worse the pain, the more your ability to act is restricted. Know that even a minor ache in the forearms can handicap you for months or even years. To convince you of this, ask others who have more years of training than you do. Doing this could help you in the long run.

To prevent this type of pain, you have at your disposal a combination of three strategies that should be used simultaneously:

❶ Warm up this zone very well before any training by squeezing a hand grip strengthener or a soft ball.

❷ Strengthen the extensor muscles using strength training exercises (see Exercises for Golf and Sports Involving Rotation on p. 100).

❸ Do myofascial massage so as to accelerate recovery between workouts (see Exercises for Golf and Sports Involving Rotation on p. 100).

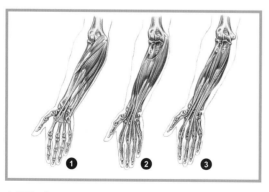

▲ Wrist flexor muscles:
❶ Superficial layer
❷ Middle layer
❸ Deep layer

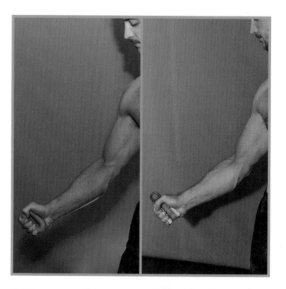

▲ It is very easy to warm up and strengthen these muscles using a hand grip strengthener so as to prevent golf elbow.

REESTABLISH SYMMETRY

Golf is the perfect example of an asymmetric sport, so you might wonder if you can strengthen your golf swing by doing strength training exercises using rotations only on the same side as your swing. Similarly, if the finger and wrist extensor muscles are normally sore after golf, why not just work to strengthen them and not the antagonistic muscles? It seems that the major asymmetries fostered by these types of sports are an important factor in injuries. But, via strength training, you can reestablish the major strength balance between the muscles of the right and left sides and between the agonists and antagonists. When your body is more balanced, it will be better able to express its full power and will be better protected against injury.

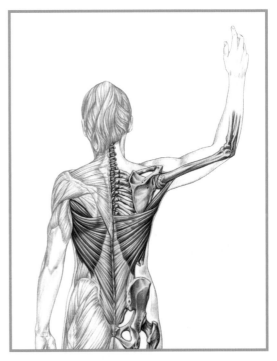

▲ Latissimus dorsi and teres major muscles.

SEE ALSO

Specific programs for golf are provided for you in the last part of this book (see listing of various programs on p. 158). Refer to the strength training exercises for the latissimus dorsi and the shoulders (see Exercises for Swimming and Nautical Sports on p. 111), because these muscles, working synergistically with the obliques, help increase the power of your swing. It might also be important to strengthen your entire leg to increase your stability (see Exercises for Running Sports on p. 66 and Exercises for Team Ball Sports on p. 93).

SWIMMING AND NAUTICAL SPORTS

These kinds of sports usually require a powerful back. We will see how to strengthen it in the second part of this book. However, just as for runners, you have to understand how morphology, and especially bone structure, influence the ability to perform in aquatic sports. They also affect the risk of injury. We will therefore study the injuries that result from intensive use of the deltoids. Strengthening the shoulders as well as the muscles that protect them is essential for participating in sports where the arms make large circles.

MUSCLES USED IN SWIMMING

Generally, the longer a swimmer's arms and the bigger the hands, the harder the back muscles and the backs of the shoulders will have to work. Therefore, they must be strong. Additionally, the wider the shoulders are, the less stable they are and the greater the risk of overuse injuries. So it is necessary to strengthen the rotator muscles of the shoulder as well as the muscles that support the shoulder blades.

For powerful leg movements, you must work on your glutes, hamstrings, rectus femoris, and psoas muscles (see Exercises for Running Sports on p. 66).

Since this is an endurance sport where breathing is obstructed, some athletes will need to improve their pulmonary capacity by working the diaphragm.

▲ The long head of the triceps is the only part of this muscle that is polyarticular, and it acts powerfully, working together with the back muscles, to bring the arm back along the torso. It is important to strengthen it using specific strength training exercises.

SWIMMING, ENDURANCE, AND BONE FRAGILITY

Medical research has shown that, among athletes, bone mineral density (which indicates how solid the bones are) is overall very poor in swimmers.[1] More generally, endurance athletes have the most fragile bones. In long-distance runners, bone fragility in men is greater than that in women, which represents a notable exception in the field of sports. Compared to strength training practitioners, whose bone density reaches 1.44 grams per square centimeter, swimmers and long-distance runners have a bone density of only 1.27 grams per square centimeter. Strength training represents an effective and quick way to counteract this bone fragility. However, it is a double-edged sword, because the more muscle you have, the less well you float. Swimmers must strive to improve their strength and endurance all while minimizing any gains in muscle mass.

THE DIFFERENT MORPHOLOGICAL ASSETS OF GOOD SWIMMERS

Even though the best swimmers have similar morphologies, there are differences depending on their specialty.

Butterfly

All swimmers have broad shoulders, but this is even more true for those who do the butterfly. So that the arms have the largest possible range of motion, the shoulder blades must also be very mobile.

Crawl

This stroke does not require the shoulders to be as large and as mobile as does the butterfly. However, the pelvis must be able to oscillate very easily.

Breaststroke

In the breaststroke, a swimmer must have excellent range of motion in the hips. To achieve this, good bone structure is a prerequisite, with a femur head that is naturally oriented to the outside. The rotator muscles of the hips (see Team Ball Sports on p. 36) must be strong and the adductors must be powerful (see Racquet and Throwing Sports on p. 54). The pectoral muscles play a more important role in bringing the arms to the body than in other swim strokes (see Racquet and Throwing Sports on p. 54).

Backstroke

Possessing good shoulder mobility is key for generating a long, powerful stroke, by getting arms into an efficient overhead position when entering the water. Backstrokers also need to have good ankle mobility since the kick is so much different than that of say, flyers, due to the increased longitudinal rotation.

Shoulder Impingement Syndrome

Shoulder pain is frequent in all sports that require you to lift your arms in the air. It occurs especially often in swimmers, as well as in athletes who do sports that involve throwing or who play golf or even volleyball.

The supraspinatus tendon and its muscle are the main victims of what doctors call impingement syndrome. To understand fully what this means, you have to first understand that the supraspinatus has two major functions:

❶ It participates, along with the other rotator cuff muscles, in maintaining the stability of the humerus when the shoulder begins to move.

❷ It participates in raising the arm to the side.

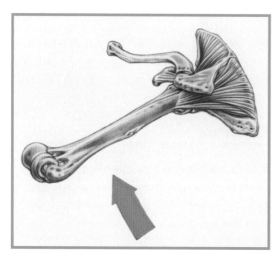

▲ When you lift your arm, particularly over your head, the infraspinatus tendon can strike the acromion. In athletes, the incessant repetition of this movement creates microtraumas, which accumulate over time and can end up causing pain. This pain can be debilitating.

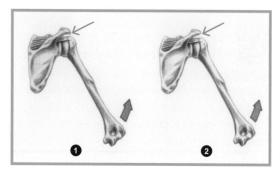

❶ The bigger the acromion, the smaller the arm's range of motion and the greater the risk of injury.

❷ The smaller the acromion, the greater the range of motion for the arm; this provides an advantage, especially when coupled with good shoulder blade mobility. But not everyone has such a range of motion. We do not recommend that you attempt the range of motion you see in a champion athlete if your bone structure does not allow for it since this will guarantee very premature overuse of your shoulders.

A Provoked Syndrome

Instead of happening naturally, this syndrome can also be caused by the head of the humerus moving higher and toward the front. This movement artificially reduces the subacromial space and promotes friction on the supraspinatus tendon. It is caused by muscle imbalances that happen when athletic training is not followed by rebalancing strength training exercises.

Premature fatigue in the protector muscles during athletic activity is also a cause. Though the muscles protect the shoulder perfectly at the beginning of athletic activity, the situation can grow progressively worse the more tired you become. The proper position for rotating the shoulder could be compromised.[2,3]

The more vulnerable the protector muscles are to fatigue, the worse the resulting shoulder injuries can be. Strength training should allow you to increase not only the strength of the protective muscles, but also their endurance, to achieve maximum effectiveness.

STRENGTH TRAINING TO OVERCOME SHOULDER PAIN

Recentering the shoulder, by working the muscles that pull the shoulder backward (back of the shoulder, middle trapezius, infraspinatus, and rhomboids) will provide tremendous relief for an athlete suffering from shoulder pain. Studies show that, among swimmers, four weeks of strength training for the rotator cuff muscles done three times each week increased the subacromial space, thus reducing the risk of shoulder impingement syndrome.[4]

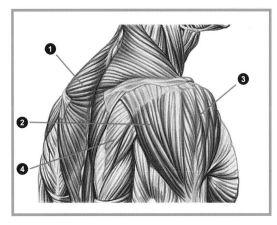

❶ Trapezius
❷ Posterior heads of the deltoid
❸ Middle part of the deltoid
❹ Infraspinatus

Which Strength Training Exercise Is Best for the Shoulders' Protective Muscles?

We are not talking about doing all available strength training exercises for the rotator cuff. Some are more appropriate for a quick warm-up before athletic practice or before strength training. To strengthen these muscles, you can find the arm position that is the closest to what you use in your sport. If you have shoulder pain during an exercise, try the variations listed with the main exercise in the second part of this book. These will allow you to develop stronger muscles without causing pain.

SEE ALSO

All movements in which the torso rotates are covered in the chapter Golf and Sports Involving Rotation (see p. 43). Hip rotation is explained in Team Ball Sports (see p. 36). Finally, we discuss strength training for the thighs in the chapters Running Sports, Cycling and Road Sports, and Combat Sports (see pp. 12, 57, and 61).

RACQUET AND THROWING SPORTS

Racquet and throwing sports, as well as ball sports where you have to throw the ball with the hands or the arms (such as handball or volleyball), have similarities in regard to the ideal morphology. They also have similar movements, and because of this, the same muscles are recruited. This means that these muscles can be strengthened in a similar way too. But these similarities are not limited to positive aspects; there are obviously also similar causes of injuries.

There is also another problem, common in tennis but present in many other activities requiring use of the hands: pain on the outside of the forearm. This is the famous tennis elbow. We will show you how strength training can help you avoid this.

IDEAL MORPHOLOGY

The Ideal Torso Morphology

To throw or strike well, it is better to have large arms, good mobility in the deltoids and shoulder blades, and large shoulders. These characteristics give you a good chance of going far and transferring the maximum amount of power to the object thrown.

The upper torso shown here, which resembles that of a swimmer, can suffer the same types of shoulder injuries seen in a swimmer. Refer to the chapter Swimming and Nautical Sports (p. 50) to learn more; to find strengthening exercises to prevent injuries, read Exercises for Swimming and Nautical Sports (p. 111).

▲ Even if it seems that only the lower part of the body is working, all the muscles are used to throw an object.

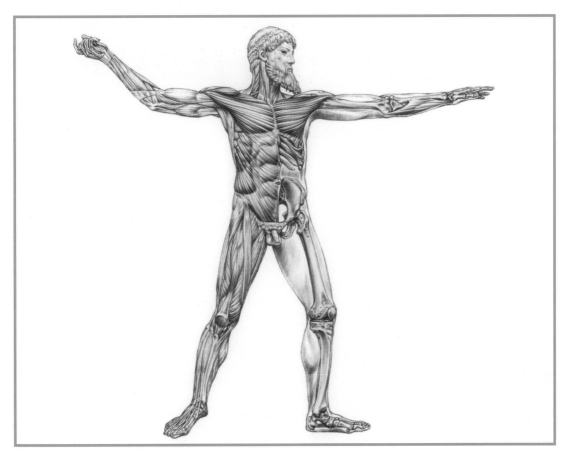

▲ During throwing, a powerful torso can store energy better and also better transmit elastic muscle strength.

The Ideal Leg Morphology

In throwing sports, athletes' legs are reminiscent of those of sprinters, except for their calves, which are a little more muscled to ensure that starts and stops are as dynamic as possible (see Running Sports on p. 12). But, in contrast to sprinters who run in a straight line with no obstacle in the way, in racquet and throwing sports you must run in all directions and make plenty of abrupt stops. This causes even more injuries than team ball sports. In addition to Achilles' tendon ruptures and injuries to the hip rotator muscles, the adductors can suffer severe trauma. You must strengthen them if you want to avoid strains or even tears.

Size of the Limbs and Range of Motion

In most sports, and especially in ball sports like volleyball or basketball, athletes with long arms and long legs have the advantage. However, the longer your arms and thighs, the larger the range of motion you have during strength training exercises. You might wonder if it is a good idea to exploit this larger range of motion.

Contrary to the popular belief that only the biggest possible movements are effective, we think that the bigger athletes are, the more careful they must be about using the full range of motion, especially in pushing exercises like squats, leg presses, deadlifts, and shoulder presses. The reason? The longer the limbs are, the more intense the stretch will be, and it could be dangerous when one is using heavy weights. Furthermore, the contraction loses its intensity at the top of the movement over a bigger range of motion.

If you are tall, it is prudent to reduce your range of motion, especially during the stretching phase, to decrease the risks associated with the exercise. Adding resistance bands to the bar or the machine is particularly beneficial for tall people to help them avoid nonproductive and dangerous zones. This tip lets you
❶ lighten the weight as you lower the bar or the machine, reducing the danger during the stretch, and
❷ minimize the unproductive zone where tension is lacking as you straighten your arms or legs.

ELBOW PAIN AND TENNIS ELBOW

Throwing sports and tennis put the ligaments of the elbow as well as the forearm muscles to the test. Strengthening the finger and wrist extensor muscles reduces the stress placed on these ligaments and tendons with each throw, and this helps prevent injuries.[1] Many strength training exercises are specifically devoted to these muscles in the chapter Exercises for Racquet and Throwing Sports (p. 125).

We strongly recommend that you not restrict yourself solely to work on the extensor muscles, but that you also focus on the flexor muscles so that your strength remains balanced (see Golf and Sports Involving Rotation on p. 43). In the same way, even if you use only your right hand, we recommend that you work the left hand just as hard during strength training, always with the goal of maintaining balance within the body.

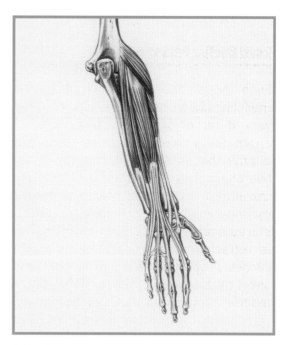

▲ Tennis elbow is nothing other than golf elbow (see Golf and Sports Involving Rotation on p. 43) that affects the extensor muscles of the wrist and finger instead of the flexor muscles.

CYCLING AND ROAD SPORTS

Cycling is probably the sport with the widest variation in muscle mass as a function of the distances covered. Some riders have enormous thighs, while long-distance cyclists usually try to reduce their muscle mass so they weigh less and can pedal faster. However, no matter what the distance is, scientific studies show that strength training can improve performance so long as the training is specifically designed for the physical qualities needed by the cyclist for the distance covered.

After first analyzing the ideal muscle morphology for cyclists, we will discuss the benefits that strength training can provide. Finally, we will examine the problem of back pain, which occurs frequently in cyclists because of the leaning-forward position. Of course, back pain also occurs quite often in many other athletes.

THE IDEAL MORPHOLOGY OF A CYCLIST

Road Cyclist Versus a Sprinter

Even though they use nearly the same muscles, these two disciplines do so in very different ways. Sprinters use an enormous amount of released elastic energy that is stored during the negative phase of the movement. This eccentric phase is practically absent in road cycling, which means the ability to release stored energy is nearly nonexistent. This is reflected in the musculature of the cyclist: A sprinter has long tendons and short muscles while a road cyclist needs longer muscles and shorter tendons.

Damping Forces

Damping force, or negative force, becomes very important in cycling done on rough terrain. However, a road cyclist must absorb all of the shocks without being able to use this force to pedal farther. The same is true for motocross, for example, where this same type of strength in the thighs is very important for avoiding falls.

THE EFFECTS OF STRENGTH TRAINING ON A CYCLIST'S ENDURANCE

The Benefits of Strength Training

The ability of strength training to increase endurance and decrease the energy used during cycling is less than in running (see Running Sports on p. 12), because a cyclist does not store as much elastic energy as a runner. Still, in many cycling activities, even those involving endurance, anaerobic strength plays a role in performance. It is necessary, for example, when one is climbing a very steep hill, in time trials, or during the final sprint. It is also universally recognized that strength work is important to become a good hill climber.

Studies have also shown, surprisingly, that strength training can help high-level cyclists increase their pedaling economy (the equivalent of running economy for a cyclist), which reduces their energy expenditure. In champion cyclists, eight weeks of strength training (20 minutes of half squats with heavy weights, two or three times per week) in addition to their usual training improved their pedaling economy by 5 percent.[1] Strength during squats increased by 14 percent. In a race done at full aerobic capacity, fatigue decreased by 17 percent.

Strength training also helps counter another factor that limits a cyclist's progress. The strength of the muscle fibers, or endurance, actually decreases during exclusive endurance training on a bike. Replacing a little bike training with strength training restores strength to the fibers. This decreases the number of muscle fibers that a cyclist must use to produce a given effort.[2,3,4] Since fewer fibers are required, energy is conserved, and fatigue sets in later.

The Position on the Bike Changes Muscle Recruitment

There are numerous potential angles between the torso and the femur that change as you adjust your seated position on a bike, and these affect which muscles are recruited. The farther a cyclist leans forward into an aerodynamic position, the more the glutes and hamstrings work compared to the quadriceps. In fact, the more the thigh is bent, the less powerful the quadriceps will be and the more the body will have to use other muscles (glutes and hamstrings) to support the front of the thigh. In contrast, straightening the back decreases the recruitment of the glutes and makes the quadriceps work harder.

In the so-called *danseuse* position (riding out of the saddle, standing up), the quadriceps are much stronger, because the cyclist is benefitting from good levers when the legs are nearly straight. This efficient transmission also allows the cyclist to use body weight to press more firmly on the pedals. The same is true when one is using semistraight legs on the pedals to reduce shock, as is the case in cyclocross or in all-terrain biking.

Whether or not you pull with your thighs to bring the pedals back determines whether you need to work the muscles that lift the knee: tibialis anterior, rectus femoris, and psoas (see Exercises for Running Sports on p. 66).

In the same way, the position of the thighs and torso greatly affects how the calves work. If you pedal more with straight legs, then you need to work the calf in positions in which the leg is almost straight. In contrast, if you usually pedal with bent legs, then you need to focus on the soleus muscle over the gastrocnemius, by working the calf from a seated position (see Exercises for Running Sports on p. 66, focusing on the calves).

Bike Position Affects Strength Training Strategies

To strengthen the muscles when you are in a low, seated position, it is better to do vertical leg presses. For a higher seated position or to increase your strength in the *danseuse* position, choose 45-degree leg presses (see Exercises for Running Sports on p. 66).

Often, a cyclist alternates between these two positions. In that case, we recommend doing one workout with horizontal leg presses and doing vertical leg presses in the next session. But we do not recommend that you do both types of presses in the same workout to try to save time; these exercises are very similar and there are other, very different muscles that need work too.

Variations in position, as well as their respective importance, should also be reflected in your choice of strength training exercises for the thighs. In fact, for any given exercise, the range of motion used affects the strength transfer from which you can benefit. The straighter your legs are while cycling, the smaller the range of motion you should use during strength training; the less straight the legs are, the larger the range of motion should be.

Torso Work

For a sprinter who climbs hills in the *danseuse* position, there is real work happening in the elbow with the triceps to support part of the body weight and balance the bike from side to side. In mountain or all-terrain biking, the arms, just like the thighs, help absorb shock using the triceps, the front of the shoulders, and the pectoral muscles to handle the bumps and changes in terrain. Some cyclists need to strengthen these zones.

Back Pain

Because of their position, especially if they are riding on rough terrain, cyclists often have low back pain. You see the same kinds of injuries in skiers and motorcycle riders too, but most athletes are affected by back pain regardless of their sport.

Pain can also occur in the upper back. In that case, it is important to focus your strength training efforts on the muscles that stabilize the shoulder blades so that they will have greater endurance (see Exercises for Swimming and Nautical Sports on p. 111). Other than back issues, piriformis syndrome (affecting the pyramidalis or piriformis muscles) affects long-distance runners, golfers, and race car drivers as well as cyclists. This kind of pain is often confused with sciatica, because the pain radiates through the glute and thigh. To prevent it, we recommend warming up the hip rotator muscles very well before any physical activity (see Exercises for Team Ball Sports on p. 93, as well the programs in part III listed on p. 158). For cyclists, forgetting to warm up these muscles is associated with a greater incidence of overuse pain in the knees.[5]

How to Combat Bone Demineralization

Medical analyses done during a competition season showed that cyclists' bone mass tended to worsen. For example, competitors in the Tour de France had bone mineral densities that were 10 percent less than in sedentary men of the same age.[6] Cycling is one of the sports in which bone mineral density is less than that of sedentary people even though the sport is supposed to strengthen bones. This fragility is especially pronounced in the hips and the spine, and this only increases the risk of low back pain.

This demineralization not only affects health; it becomes problematic during a fall since it increases the risk of serious bone fractures in cyclists. Doing a little strength training regularly can reverse this tendency, offering benefits not only in the short term for the athlete's health, but also in the long term since age increases the risk of osteopenia.[7] Specific programs to strengthen bone are provided in the third part of this book.

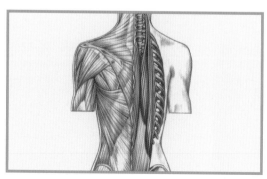

▲ For all athletes, it is a good idea to strengthen the muscles that protect the spine and to decompress the back after every workout.

COMBAT SPORTS

More than any other discipline, combat sports, especially mixed martial arts (MMA), recruit all the muscles of the body. All muscle qualities—explosiveness, power, strength, flexibility, and endurance—are required. A fighter's training is therefore tedious, especially if you add in the physical preparation involved in learning combat techniques.

We have devoted an entire book to specific strength training for fighting[1] and we invite you to read it for more detailed information. In the second part of this book, we will offer you some new exercises that can help fighters change the balance of power, especially during ground fighting, so that the opponent's weight will not be an obstacle. The lighter your opponent seems, the easier it will be to dominate that opponent. Additionally, given the degree of risk of injuries in a fight, we will also focus on exercises whose common objective is to prevent injury.

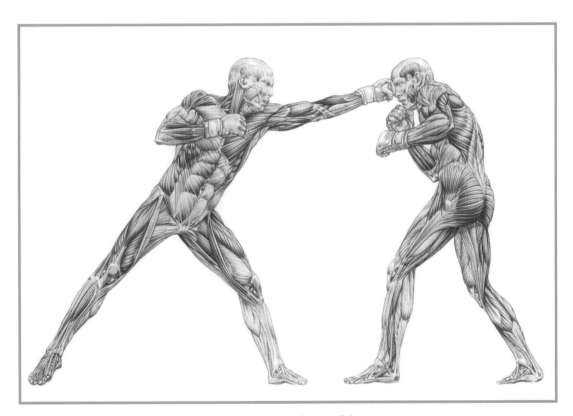

▲ There are few sports in which the risk of injury is as high as during a fight.

The incidence of injury in combat sports is very high. Statistics show that more than half of athletes who participate regularly in these sports suffer injuries within a year.[2] Unlike the situation in noncontact sports, we are talking not only about overuse injuries, but also impacts and hyperextension of the tendons and ligaments.[2] In the long term, the goals of regular strength training are to make you stronger and to strengthen the tendons as well as the ligaments. In the short term, there are two goals:

❶ Get into the habit of warming up these tissues well before each workout since the majority of injuries occur in training, not during competitions.[2]

❷ Accelerate recovery and regeneration between workouts, which is problematic when you have to do your training sessions one after the other.

These two goals are more difficult to attain than it would seem, because there is less blood flow to the tendons and ligaments compared to the muscles. Thus, our strategy is to bring the most blood possible to these poorly irrigated regions. We achieve this through exercises done with very light resistance bands in very long sets (between 100 and 200 reps). Rather than adding boring workout sessions that involve multiple sets, we stick to brief, daily workouts that you can do at home.

Support for the Neck and Shoulder Blades

The neck and shoulders are vulnerable areas during a fight, not only because of the blows received, but also because of falls. The only way to protect them is to cover them with muscle.

Imbalance Between the Quadriceps and the Hamstrings

As in runners, we find the classic strength imbalance between the quadriceps and the hamstrings (which are much too weak).

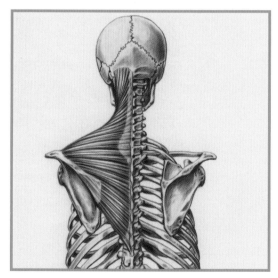

▲ The upper-trapezius muscles, which climb up the neck, act like muscular armor for the cervical vertebrae. The middle trapezius muscles stabilize the shoulders by holding the shoulder blades. Strengthening this area pulls the deltoids backward, improving posture and recentering the humerus in the glenoid cavity (thus reducing the risk of injury). This is very useful for preventing shoulder pain, not only in combat sports but also in all sports that require heavy use of the arms (such as swimming or throwing).

This imbalance does not optimize performance, especially because there is less stability in the legs. In addition, it increases the risk of injury, particularly in the knees.[3] The first two exercises covered in the chapter Exercises for Combat Sports (see p. 144) are appropriate for recalibrating the strength of these antagonistic muscles.

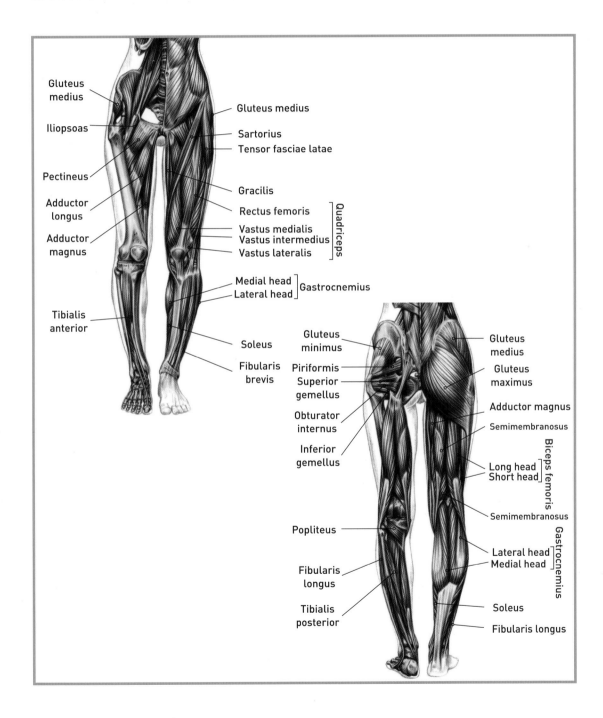

Gluteus medius
Iliopsoas
Pectineus
Adductor longus
Adductor magnus
Tibialis anterior

Gluteus medius
Sartorius
Tensor fasciae latae
Gracilis
Rectus femoris
Vastus medialis
Vastus intermedius
Vastus lateralis
Quadriceps
Medial head
Lateral head
Gastrocnemius
Soleus
Fibularis brevis

Gluteus minimus
Piriformis
Superior gemellus
Obturator internus
Inferior gemellus
Popliteus
Fibularis longus
Tibialis posterior

Gluteus medius
Gluteus maximus
Adductor magnus
Semimembranosus
Long head
Short head
Biceps femoris
Semimembranosus
Lateral head
Medial head
Gastrocnemius
Soleus
Fibularis longus

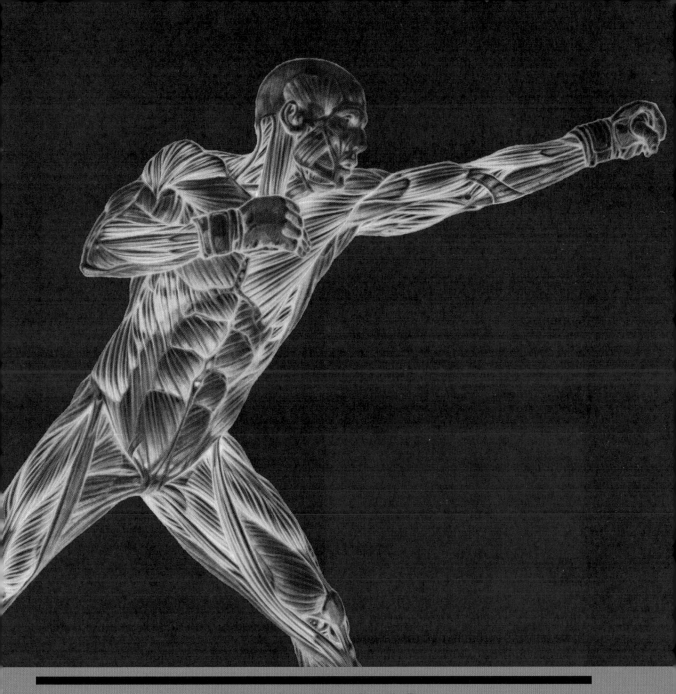

EXERCISES
FOR
EVERY SPORT

EXERCISES FOR RUNNING SPORTS

POWER RUNNER

Why Should an Athlete Do This Exercise?

This basic exercise works all the muscles of the lower body that propel the leg backward. It rather faithfully reproduces the starting position for a sprint.

For Which Sports?

This exercise is appropriate for all sports in which you must sprint or start a run abruptly. It is also useful for cyclists, especially track cyclists.

In the machine, place your head between the two padded cushions and block your shoulders. Grab the handles for stability. Lift one leg and place the foot on the pedal ❶. Do the same with the other foot. Keep your back very straight and push on one leg as you let the knee of the other leg move forward ❷. Continue doing strides until you reach fatigue.

Notes

Work in the most explosive manner possible. Adding a resistance band will make the exercise more dynamic.

Advantages

Working the thighs in this way is true to physiology because of the circular and asymmetric trajectory, just like when you run.

Disadvantages

Though the muscles that move the leg backward are perfectly stimulated, the same is not true about the muscles that lift the knee. So you need to strengthen them using other specific exercises.

⚠ Risks

The back is under more intense pressure than it experiences during running. We recommend that you use a weight belt to protect your lumbar spine.

LUNGE

Why Should an Athlete Do This Exercise?

A basic exercise, lunges have a lot in common with one-legged squats, and they work the entire thigh.

For Which Sports?

Lunges are good for athletes who use their thighs asynchronously, like runners, cyclists, and fencers.

Stand with your feet close together and straight legs, with your hands resting on your hips or thighs. Begin the exercise by taking a large step forward with the left leg, and then return to the starting position. Either repeat on the same leg or switch to the other leg.

Notes

The farther you lean your torso forward, the more the hamstrings and glutes are recruited. The straighter your back is, the more the quadriceps have to work. Finally, the larger the range of motion in the exercise, the more the glutes and the backs of the thighs have to work. A smaller range of motion will better target the quadriceps.

To add resistance, you can

✪ straighten the leg that is in the back, or
✪ hold a weight in the hands or on the shoulders.

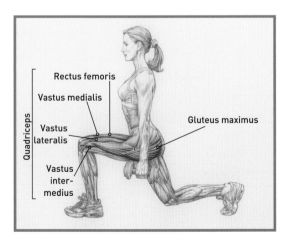

Rectus femoris
Vastus medialis
Quadriceps
Vastus lateralis
Gluteus maximus
Vastus intermedius

Variations

A Lunging on a bench makes the exercise harder.

B You can jump into the air with each lunge as you change legs. This will improve both your ability to stop and your explosiveness. Just as you work on acceleration, you should also work on deceleration when doing strength training since you use eccentric force to put the "brakes" on the muscle. The stronger your muscles are eccentrically, the better you will be able to stop or to reduce your speed rapidly while abusing your joints as little as possible (therefore sparing them from injury and avoiding dangerous angles). You will also be able to start again quickly, in an explosive manner.

C Instead of doing a forward lunge, do a side lunge. Side lunges are similar to the muscular work required in sports where you have to move to the side, for example, in ball sports, racquet sports, or martial arts.

D To increase resistance during side lunges, place a resistance band around your hips and attach the other end to a fixed point somewhere to the side at about the midpoint of the working leg.

E Using a machine lets you change the degree of resistance during the exercise.

Advantages

Lunges work the entire thigh, at home or on the go, with little equipment required. They are less violent than squats or deadlifts since they do not compress the spine as much as those exercises.

The farther the knee goes beyond the foot, the harder the patella has to work. Protect your knees by landing gently on the ground and using your calves to absorb the shock. Be careful not to lose your balance, especially as your muscles get tired.

Why Should an Athlete Do This Exercise?

This basic exercise targets the entire thigh, but we recruit the glutes and hamstrings with an original stretching angle by modifying the position of the feet.

For Which Sports?

This is for any sport that uses the upper hamstrings so intensely that they have a high risk of tearing, as in running, for example.

▲ A 45-degree leg press in the classic position.

■ VERTICAL LEG PRESS

Lie on your back on the cushion and press your back into it. Lift one leg and then the other and place your feet on the platform ❶. Once you are stable, release the safety brackets and lower the platform. When your quadriceps brush your torso ❷, straighten your legs and then repeat the movement. The vertical leg press works the hamstrings and the glutes much more than any other leg press.

■ HORIZONTAL OR 45-DEGREE LEG PRESS

On a 45-degree leg press machine, using a high foot position allows you to reproduce the muscle recruitment you experience during a vertical press. Adjust the seat so that it is parallel to the foot platform. Place your feet as high as possible on the platform, but not so high that it becomes uncomfortable. Release the safety brackets, if any, and lower the platform. When your quadriceps brush your torso ❶, straighten your legs ❷ and repeat.

Points to Consider

The wider apart you place your feet, the lower your legs will come down before brushing your torso; this will give you a better stretch in the back of the thighs and the adductors.

TIP

Some press machines let an athlete work the thighs asynchronously, reproducing the type of movement found in running. This is often the case for horizontal presses.

Notes

Begin by lowering the thighs with control so that your hamstrings have time to get used to the intense stretch provided by this movement. As you progress, you can go lower and lower instead of using heavier weight.

Advantages

When the feet are placed up high, the press gives you a unique angle of attack for the muscles and works the entire thigh in a single exercise. This is what runners are looking for, because it focuses the work on the glutes and especially the hamstrings.

⚠ Risks

The more you arch your back, the bigger the range of motion will be, and the more you can feel the contraction. But this comes at a price; you are also putting the discs in your lumbar spine at risk.

GLUTE-HAM RAISE (GHR), RAZOR CURL, AND NORDIC HAMSTRING CURL

Why Should an Athlete Do These Exercises?

✪ These three exercises, which are body weight movements, are rather similar since they start from the same position: feet blocked in the ankle hooks for support and to create a lever to lift the torso using the hamstrings. These exercises will strengthen the hamstrings, with the all-important goal of preventing injuries.

✪ Though Nordic hamstring curls are a monoarticular exercise that mobilizes only the knees, razor curls and GHRs are biarticular exercises since they mobilize the hips and the knees. Begin with the easiest variation (GHRs) before moving to the more advanced exercises (razor curls and Nordic hamstring curls).

For Which Sports?

These are for any sport that requires running and jumping.

■ GHR

Begin on your knees, with your feet locked into the ankle hooks on a GHR bench. Place your hands on your chest and lean forward until your torso is perpendicular to the ground ❶. Push with the tips of your feet and pull with your hamstrings, glutes, and low back at the same time to lift your torso until it is parallel to the ground and forms a straight line with your legs. From there, bend your knees so that the back of your thighs and your back form nearly a 90-degree angle with the calves ❷. So as to maintain continuous tension in your muscles, do not come all the way to 90 degrees. Without stopping, lower all the way back down. If this exercise seems too hard at first, use your hands to help you by pushing on the bench.

To make it easier to lift your torso, your knees can slide toward the ground against the knee pad, which provides a counterbalance to the body.

Notes

Thanks to CrossFit, GHR benches are more and more common in gyms, which opens up a range of new exercises. They have many advantages:

✪ On these benches, you can do classic GHRs, razor curls, or Nordic hamstring curls. Additionally, with your torso perpendicular to the ground in the lengthened position, the exercise has a larger range of motion with a better hamstring stretch. As we have already seen, strength training exercises that stretch the muscle are the most effective for preventing hamstring tears.

✪ It is easier to place your feet wide apart on a GHR bench. The width should be the same as what you use in your sport (relatively close for those who run in a straight line or wider for those who move a lot to the side). If you need both of these widths, then do one set with the feet close together and a second set with the feet wider apart, alternating between sets.

✪ In addition to holding you by your heels, the bench allows you to push with your calves since the balls of your feet are touching the foot plate. When your feet cannot press against something solid, the isolation of the hamstrings is better, but you also lose a lot of strength. Isolation exercises for the backs of the thighs, like leg curls, do not allow you to press with the balls of your feet. Even in a deadlift, it is hard to push with the calves. Being able to push on the balls of your feet to increase your strength is a special feature of GHRs. You should take advantage of this since this combination of muscle contractions is found in running.

⚠ **Warning!**

On GHR benches, the adjustment is critical since it completely changes the difficulty of the exercise. The best adjustment is the one that is the closest to your level of strength.

■ The lower the knees are compared to the feet, the easier the exercise will be. The exercise is harder when the feet and the knees are in line so that the calves are parallel to the ground.

■ The farther the ankle hooks are placed from the knee pad, the farther down your knees can go during the contraction, and this will make it easier to lift your torso. In contrast, the closer the ankle hooks are to the knee pad, the less the knees will be able to slide down during the contraction. This means you can no longer take advantage of your own body weight during the rocking movement to lift your torso. In turn this means very intense work for your hamstrings.

■ RAZOR CURL

Begin on your knees with your heels locked into an ab bench, a seat for a high lat pulley, or a GHR bench. Sit on your calves and, if you can, place your hands on your chest ❶. Slowly move your torso forward and straighten out through your knees as well as your glutes so that your back is eventually in line with your legs ❷. At first, do not move your glutes too far away from your calves, because the farther forward you move your torso, the harder the exercise becomes. When you are strong enough, move your body until it is parallel to the ground and then come back up using the strength in your hamstrings.

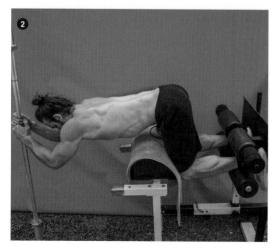

TIP

If you are not strong enough to come back up on your own, use your hands to cushion the shock of touching the ground. You can also push with your hands at the bottom of the movement to come back up if your thighs are not strong enough. Another solution is to grab the back of your thighs with your hands and use your arm strength to lift yourself back up.

Holding onto a bar in front of you will also make it easier to learn this exercise.

Notes

This version is much easier than the next one since the hamstrings are a polyarticular muscle. Instead of contracting both ends, as in Nordic hamstring curls, the muscle on the back of the thigh contracts at the knees while being stretched at the hips during the positive phase and inversely during the negative phase. This makes the hamstrings much stronger.[1]

■ NORDIC HAMSTRING CURL

Begin on your knees with your heels locked into an ab bench, a seat for a high lat pulley, or a GHR bench. Place your hands on your chest with your thighs perpendicular to your calves so that your hamstrings are in line with your back ❶. Lean your torso forward while keeping your back in line with your thighs, first just an inch or so, and then you can go farther ❷. When you get stronger, you can touch the ground with your hands before using your hamstrings to pull yourself back up.

Points to Consider

The arm position greatly affects the difficulty of this exercise. It is easier with your arms alongside your body and much harder with your hands crossed behind your head or even holding a weight behind your head.

Note that the knees are blocked by the knee pad, which means you cannot use your body as a counterweight to easily lift your torso. Move gradually and carefully. Do not let yourself be pulled by your own body weight because, past a certain point, you will not be strong enough to lift yourself back up. If this happens, use your hands to catch yourself before hitting the ground. You can also push with your hands at the bottom of the movement to come back up if your thighs are not strong enough.

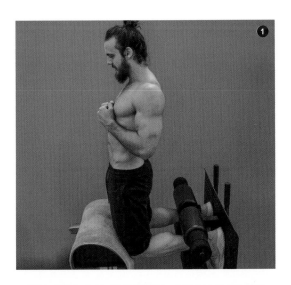

Variations

A Without equipment or on the go, a partner can replace the bench by holding your feet.

B Some benches allow you, when necessary, to assist yourself with your arms by pushing on the ground.

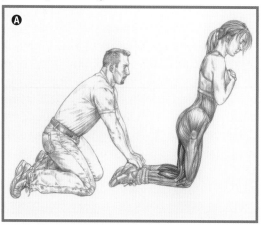

Advantages

These are exercises in which you can do just the descent, thereby doing only the negative phase of the exercise, which can strengthen the hamstrings and prevent injury, or you can do it as a form of reeducation after a tear. You can use your hands to come back up if you want to avoid the positive phase of the exercise or if this phase is too hard. It is up to you to determine the level of stretch in the negative phase depending on how far you lower your torso. In case of injury or if you are a beginner, start with a limited range of motion (and stretch) that you can gradually increase over time.

Disadvantages

If you do not have a GHR bench, you must have a good cushion for the knees since this exercise places a lot of mechanical pressure on the patella.

⚠ Risks

Begin cautiously and move gradually. Do not let your body weight pull you around. Be sure that your calves are locked in firmly, either in the machine or held by your partner, because if they move, you will fall!

PULL THROUGH

Why Should an Athlete Do This Exercise?

This exercise mobilizes the hip joints and, to some extent, the knees as well. It targets numerous muscle groups, like the hamstrings, the glutes, and the back. The goal is to get your hamstrings used to being stretched while they are under sharp tension, which will help minimize the tears that are so frequent in this area.

For Which Sports?

This exercise is for all sports that involve running because it will strengthen the muscles of the back of the thigh, primarily the upper part.

With a low pulley behind your back, grab the handle with both hands. Take one step forward, perhaps a few, so that you can lower your torso without the weight touching the stacked weights on the machine. Spread your legs at least shoulder-width apart and lean your torso as far forward ❶ as your hamstring flexibility allows. Once you have reached the low position, raise your torso ❷. Ideally, you should keep your body slightly leaning forward so that it is never completely perpendicular to the ground.

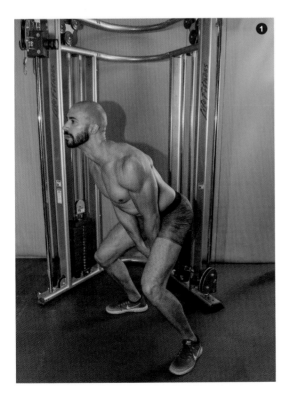

Variations

Ⓐ You can do this exercise with completely straight or slightly bent legs. You can also crouch by bending the legs to almost 90 degrees during the stretching phase and by gradually straightening them throughout the contraction. This will alter how your hamstrings work during the exercise.

Ⓑ If no pulley is available, you can attach a resistance band to a low, stationary point behind you instead.

Ⓒ This exercise can be done with a dumbbell instead of a pulley.

Ⓓ You can also use a kettlebell. Instead of keeping the weight between your legs, lift one or both hands in the air as high as possible while straightening the arms to do kettlebell swings (if you are working only one arm at a time, do not rest in between swings). This is an athletic conditioning exercise that is typically done in long sets (at least 20 reps) for strength and endurance instead of with very heavy weights as in classic strength training. The low back and the shoulders work much harder than in the other variations, which could be advantageous for volleyball, tennis, and combat sports.

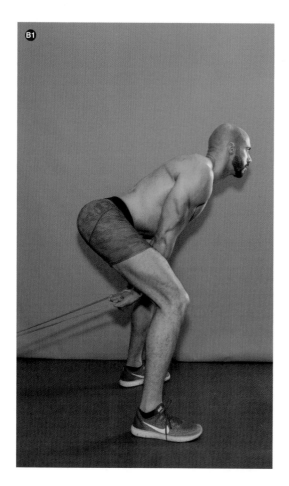

Points to Consider

You can change the degree to which various muscles are recruited. Depending on how much you voluntarily contract your glutes during the exercise, they will work more or less intensely. If you do not lean very far forward, the low back remains under more tension compared to the hamstrings. In contrast, the bigger the stretch is, the harder the hamstrings will work.

Notes

The wider apart the feet are, the easier it is to go down lower and thus increase the range of motion during the exercise. Of course, you can change the distance between your feet to modify which muscles are recruited.

Advantages

This is a good warm-up exercise with which to begin a strength training ses-sion. Even though it causes a certain amount of tension in the low back, the pressure on the discs is not even close to what you experience during exercises like the deadlift.

Disadvantages

Beyond a certain amount of weight, it gets harder to stay in place since the pulley will gradually pull you toward it. More than your strength, this is a stability problem that limits how much weight you can use. In this case, it is better to use a slightly lighter weight so that you can do more repetitions.

⚠ Risks

Just as in a deadlift, you will be stronger with your back arched than with your back straight. But that position is also riskier for your discs. So force yourself to keep your spine very straight, even if it means that you have to lean your torso a little less forward.

Why Should an Athlete Do This Exercise?

These isolation exercises recruit the hamstrings, especially the lower part, near the knee.

For Which Sports?

These are for all sports that involve running or jumping.

Select a weight and get onto the machine (lying on your belly). Position your ankles under the cushioned ankle brace and use your hamstrings to bring your feet toward your glutes before lowering back to the lengthened position.

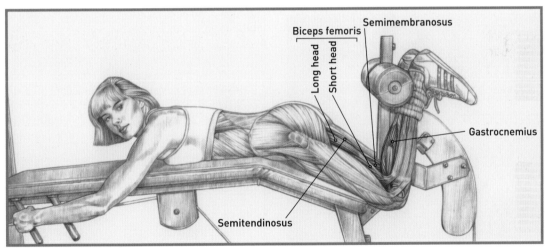

▲ Leg curl, lying down.

▲ Leg curl, seated.

Variations

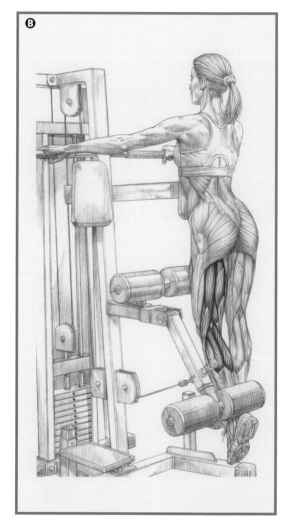

A Instead of lying down, some machines allow you to do the exercise while seated; this position is closer to the way the muscles work during a sprint. However, seated leg curls put more pressure on the cruciate ligaments in the knees. Creating unusual tension in that area can be good for strengthening it, unless your cruciate ligaments are already fatigued or damaged, in which case it is better not to traumatize them any further.

B There are standing leg curls as well. The only reason for an athlete to do them this way is that it becomes easier to work one leg as a time, in case of an injury, for example.

C If you do not have a machine, you can do leg curls by attaching a resistance band to a fixed point that is low to the ground. You can use this technique on the go to warm up the hamstrings and prepare the cruciate ligaments of the knee before a run. Similarly, doing these in long sets is a great recovery exercise.

TIP

By flexing your feet and pulling the tips of your feet toward your calves, you will feel stronger and will also work the front of your lower legs. However, if this muscle is painful, do this exercise with your feet pointed and the tips of your feet in line with your tibia to avoid recruiting the tibialis anterior.

⚠ Risks

Arching your back might make you feel stronger, but it comes at the price of compressing your lumbar spine.

Advantages

This exercise is even more important if you experience frequent injuries in your lower hamstrings. It also recruits a muscle that is difficult to strengthen: the popliteus muscle.

Disadvantages

Isolating the tension to the back of the thigh rather than the entire thigh means the knee works very hard, and this could aggravate any preexisting trauma, causing pain.

BENT-KNEE LEG LIFT

Why Should an Athlete Do This Exercise?

This basic exercise is especially good for the rectus femoris, the tensor fasciae latae, the abdominal muscles, and the psoas. The bigger your calf is and the heavier your thigh is, the more important it is to do this exercise since it recruits the muscles responsible for lifting the leg when you run, jump, or kick a ball.

For Which Sports?

This is a very important exercise for all sprinters and jumpers, and generally for all athletes who have to run.

While standing, adjust the machine so that the knee cushion is just above your knee ❶. The arm of the machine will bring your thigh more or less behind your body. Support yourself on the bar in front of you and lift your knee as high as possible ❷ as you pull in your stomach so that you are also using the strength of your abdominal muscles. Once you reach the top of the movement, lower your knee to the starting point and repeat. When you finish working on one leg, move immediately to the other leg.

Variations

A If you do not have a machine, whether you want to train at home or warm up while you are in the field, you can use a weight plate, a dumbbell, or a resistance band to provide resistance.

B Bent-knee leg lifts can be done while seated to re-create the range of motion that cyclists experience.

C Instead of lifting the foot in line with the knee, bring your heel toward the middle of your other quadriceps by rotating your hip. This works the sartorius muscle, which is very important for passing in soccer.

Advantages

When you are not at the gym, if you have knee pain or you have trouble getting your knees warmed up well before a workout, a few sets of bent-knee leg lifts can help.

Disadvantages

Working unilaterally is required in this exercise, but it does take more time. However, working one leg right after the other without resting can increase your endurance.

⚠ Risks

Do not arch your back when the leg is in the low position.

Why Should an Athlete Do This Exercise?

This isolation exercise targets the entire calf and the muscles of the bottom of the foot. Plus, strong, stiff calves help you sprint faster.[2] Studies have shown that 12 weeks of eccentric strength training for the calves increases the stiffness of the Achilles' tendon by 82 percent and muscle strength by 49 percent.[3]

For Which Sports?

This exercise is for any sport in which you use your legs to move around.

Place your feet flat on the ground, on a platform, or on a step. Push on the balls of your feet to lift your body as high as possible and then lower back down. Repeat the exercise.

TIP

You can use a belt squat type of machine to prevent compression in your low back.

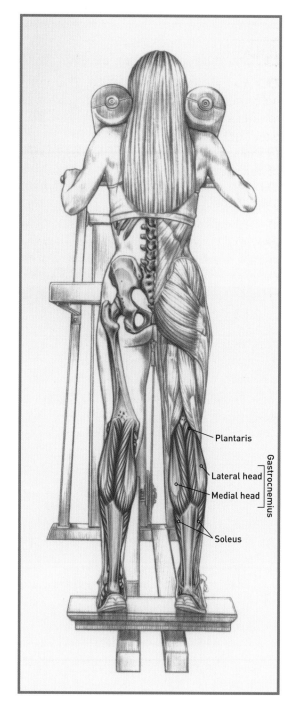

Plantaris

Lateral head — Gastrocnemius
Medial head

Soleus

Points to Consider

Adjust the space between your legs and the orientation of your feet so that the exercise feels natural for you.

Variations

Ⓐ If you do not have a machine, you can hold a dumbbell in one or in both hands to increase the resistance during this exercise.

Ⓑ Put a resistance band around the tips of your feet and hold it with your hands. The band can serve as a ballast for a warm-up in the field, or a recovery move after a workout.

Ⓒ You can also work the calves while seated in a machine.

Ⓓ Finally, you can do this exercise while crouching. Variations where you bend your legs to the maximum should, at most, constitute 10 percent of your total calf work (except in special cases like ground fighting, downhill skiing, or cycling, for example), since these variations provide less complete work than the standing version.

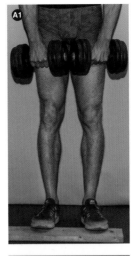

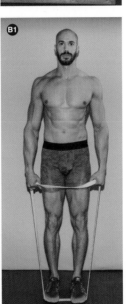

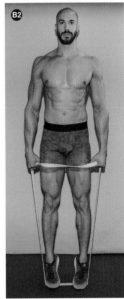

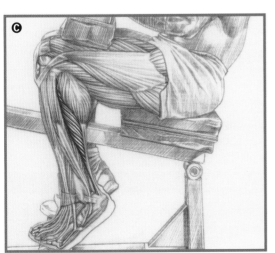

SHOULD YOU STRIVE FOR MAXIMUM RANGE OF MOTION IN THE CALVES IN STRENGTH TRAINING EXERCISES?

During strength training exercises for the calves, it is common to place the tips of the feet on a step so that you can lower your heels down as much as possible (see the photos on the left). This stretches the calves and increases the range of motion. This technique is used by bodybuilders to get the biggest muscle mass possible in the calves. But this is not necessarily a good thing for athletes. In fact, the bigger the calves are, the heavier they are and the more energy it takes to lift them. This is especially counterproductive for runners.[4]

The more tendinous your calves, the less useful the stretch at the bottom of this exercise. Runners should therefore begin the exercise on the ground or on a step that is no more than one inch high (see the photos on the right). In fact, studies show that, compared to other athletes, the best sprinters have ankles that are less flexible. Though this stiffness increases the risk of injuries, it also allows for better release of elastic energy by the calves, which increases power and saves energy. Other athletes should adjust the stretch depending on what is required in their sport. For example, cyclists need to stretch their calves a bit more, especially track cyclists.

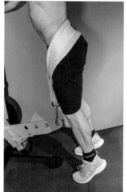
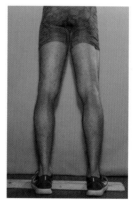
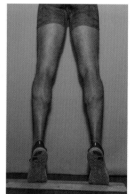

Advantages

This exercise, which works the entire calf directly, can be done anywhere since it does not require any equipment. It is ideal for warming up the Achilles' tendons before a workout or an athletic event.

Disadvantages

If your calves are naturally large, do not do this exercise too frequently. Instead, do single sets with a heavy weight and not too often.

⚠ Risks

If you add weight, you are also creating tension in your spine.

Working the calves in bare feet gives you an advantage in that you can use your toes to better anchor yourself on the ground. This means that you use more muscles, especially those in the feet. This can prove useful for certain sports, like running. In fact, the muscles on the bottom of the foot can often be a source of pain that affects every stride. Additionally, studies show that if these muscles are too weak, the risk of injuries and leg pain in runners can increase. So, even though they are small, these muscles are extremely important.[5]

If you are training at home, you can work on your calves in bare feet; often, this is not allowed in a gym.

TOWEL CURL

Why Should an Athlete Do This Exercise?

Warming up or strengthening the muscles on the bottom of the feet can prevent debilitating pain.[6]

For Which Sports?

These exercises are appropriate for all sports in which athletes use their feet to move.

Sit down with your feet flat on a large towel ❶ and bend your toes to bring the towel toward you. Once you have pulled the towel all the way toward you ❷, do the reverse movement so that you work the extensor muscles and can put the towel flat once again.

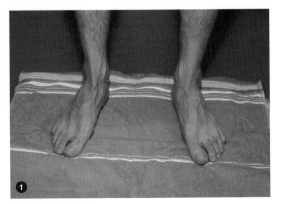

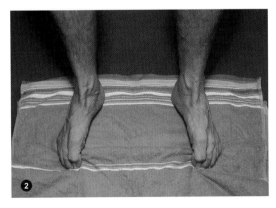

Points to Consider

After a few sessions, your mastery of this exercise will improve. You can do this exercise at any time by scrunching your toes inside your shoes 20 or 30 times. In the winter, especially if your feet are normally cold, get into the habit of doing this exercise so that you do not start a workout with "frozen" muscles.

Variation

You can do this exercise while standing to make it harder since this will greatly increase the weight resting on the feet.

Notes

Since this is only a warm-up exercise, you should stop well before your muscles grow tired.

Advantages

Isolation of the muscles is good, and you can adjust the resistance; this means you can do the exercise even if you have some pain.

Disadvantages

If you have a lot of pain, this exercise will not be very effective.

⚠ Risks

Do not do this exercise too often, especially if it takes a long time for the soles of your feet to recover between workouts.

TIP

To strengthen the muscles in the soles of your feet, begin by doing this exercise. Once your feet are tired, do standing calf raises (see p. 86 and following) to quickly strengthen these muscles. If you get sharp muscle cramps after doing this exercise, you can massage the soles of your feet with a ball to relax the muscles.

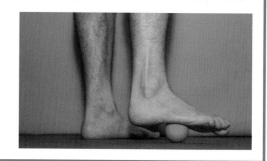

TOE RAISE

Why Should an Athlete Do This Exercise?

This exercise isolates the tibialis anterior. Often, an athlete discovers that there is a muscle on the shin only after it begins causing sharp pain.

For Which Sports?

This exercise is for all sports in which athletes could experience chronic exertional compartment syndrome. A lower leg that is strong in the shin area is useful not only in combat sports and cycling but also in soccer for shooting and passing.

Sit on a bench or a chair with your heels on the ground. Lift the top of your right foot up. Place your left foot gently on top of the right to provide resistance. As you lower your foot, use the strength in your tibialis anterior muscle to slow the descent of your right foot while the left foot is pushing on it. Once your foot is on the ground, lift the top of the left foot up and put your right foot on top. Continue the exercise as you keep switching feet.

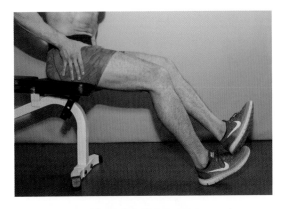

TIP

If you have muscle cramps in the shin area, it is better to massage the area with a ball to relax it than to try to strengthen it through exercise.

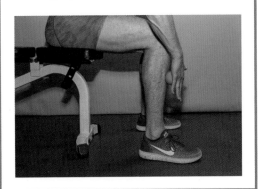

Gastrocnemius

Medial head
Lateral head

Tibialis posterior

Flexor hallucis longus

Flexor digitorum longus

Soleus

Fibularis longus

Fibularis brevis

Points to Consider

For the reasons previously mentioned, the tibialis anterior is worked only eccentrically, but it could also be worked in the classic way if you feel this is necessary.

Variations

A You can straighten or bend the legs to varying degrees to change the angle of attack for this exercise.

B Stand with your heels on a plank or on the edge of a sidewalk and lift the tips of the feet. Adding a plank under the heel increases the range of motion in the exercise and makes it harder. This exercise can serve as a warm-up before your athletic workout to help prevent injuries.

Advantages

This exercise can be done at home since it requires no equipment.

Disadvantages

This exercise should be done slowly, with perfect control, and using the largest possible range of motion. We do not recommend any explosive movement.

⚠ Risks

If you feel that this exercise is aggravating problems instead of resolving them, then skip it.

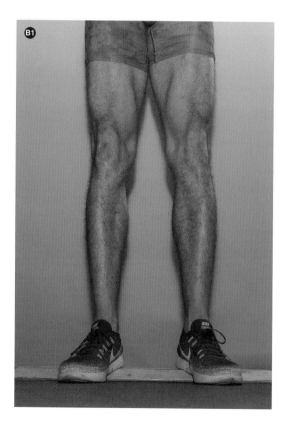

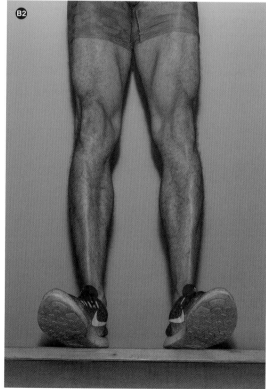

EXERCISES FOR TEAM BALL SPORTS

HIP ROTATOR WARM-UP USING A TOWEL

Why Should an Athlete Do This Exercise?

✪ Warming up the internal and external hip rotator muscles will improve performance and reduce the risk of injury to the legs.

✪ If your sport requires movement that is not in a straight line, then this warm-up is very important for you.

For Which Sports?

This exercise is for any sport in which you use your legs to move.

Place a towel on a floor that is as smooth as possible: asphalt rather than grass; a plastic, tile, or wood floor rather than carpet. If your towel is really stretched out flat, then you will need to leave some folds of towel between your feet so that your feet can move without pulling too hard on the towel.

Stand on the towel with your feet spread far enough apart that they do not touch when the tips of your feet are pointing toward each other. Use your hip rotator muscles to point the tips of your feet toward the outside ❶. Once you reach this position, then move the tips of the feet back toward each other ❷ and continue doing reps without pausing.

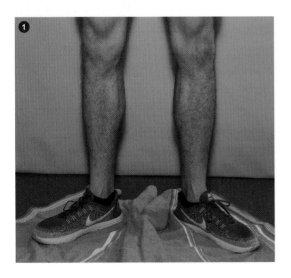

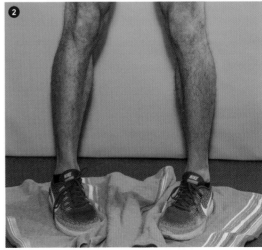

Rest your hands on your glutes so that you can better feel the hip rotator muscles moving. You should continue the set until you can really feel the muscles get warm, but not for so long that you feel even the slightest fatigue. If one set is not enough, do a second set. You should always be striving to raise your temperature, not to reach fatigue. If you feel fatigue before you get warmed up, then take 10- to 20-second pauses between sets of 10 to 20 reps. If the environment permits, do this exercise with bare feet. In this way, you can do the exercise right before or right after you warm up the muscles on the soles of your feet, by using the toes to pull the towel (see Towel Curl on p. 89).

Variation

If the standing version seems too hard or pain prevents you from doing it that way, you can do this same exercise from a seated position.

Notes

Do these rotations in a slow and controlled manner. If your feet gradually slide farther apart, just bring them back together.

Advantages

Since this warm-up requires only a smooth floor and a towel, it can be done practically anywhere before a workout. Though it offers the short-term benefit of improved performance, the long-term benefit—minimizing the risk of injuries—is what really makes a difference.

Disadvantages

This exercise can easily be added to other classic warm-up exercises, but it cannot replace them. You should also note that the rotation of the right thigh does not necessarily match that of the left thigh. Just use what nature gave you, and do not worry about making the range of motion equal for both legs.

⚠ Risks

Do not exaggerate the range of motion in this exercise, because this could put your knees in a precarious position. It is better to work with a smaller range of motion and do more repetitions. The more friction there is between the towel and the ground, the greater the risk that your knees could be placed in a poor position. This is why it is better to use a smooth floor, even for a set of 100 or 150 repetitions, rather than a rough floor that will allow you to do only a few reps.

HIP ABDUCTION

Why Should an Athlete Do This Exercise?

This exercise will build muscle in the gluteus medius and gluteus minimus.

For Which Sports?

This exercise is for all sports in which you use your legs to move.

Sit in the machine and place your legs on the inside of the two knee pads ❶. Move slowly and use the strength in your glutes to spread your legs as far apart as possible ❷. Return to the starting position just until the arms of the machine come close to each other. Do not let them touch, and then begin again.

TIP

Some machines allow you to work with straight legs and others with the legs bent to 90 degrees. You can use heavier weights with bent legs than you can with straight legs.

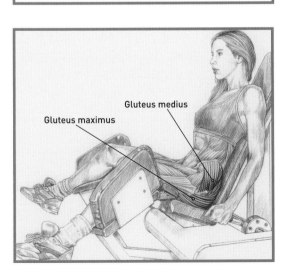

Gluteus medius

Gluteus maximus

Variations

Ⓐ Instead of sitting in the machine, you can do this exercise while standing almost all the way up, like a tennis player waiting to return a serve. This variation is valuable only if the posture is similar to the posture you use in your sport.

Ⓑ If you do not have a machine and you want to warm up on the go or train while at home, you can wrap a resistance band around your knees and do the movement while sitting on the floor in the tailor position.

Ⓒ If you do not have a resistance band, sit on a chair or on the floor and push on the upper part of your knees with your hands to provide resistance.

Advantages

This exercise strengthens crucial muscles that are often very neglected.

Disadvantages

The ability to spread the legs apart is limited. Some athletes have a greater range of motion than others. This is not just because of superior flexibility; the bony structure of the pelvis is primarily what dictates the range of motion.

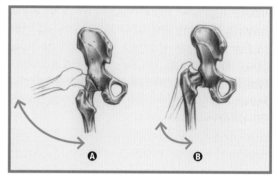

Ⓐ This pelvic bone structure provides good ability to open the legs.
Ⓑ This pelvic bone structure does not allow you to open the legs wide.

⚠ Risks

It is not a good idea to try to go beyond the natural limits imposed by your bone structure since this could damage your hip joint.

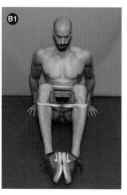

INTERNAL HIP ROTATION

Why Should an Athlete Do This Exercise?

This is an isolation exercise for all the muscles responsible for internal rotation of the femur.

For Which Sports?

This exercise is for all sports in which you to use your legs to move.

To work the internal hip rotators, use a hip abductor machine. Instead of having the moving arms of the machine in front of you, though, put them behind you. Place your knees on the seat. Hold yourself upright and lean slightly forward so that your thighs form a 90-degree angle with your calves. In this kneeling position, place your feet inside the knee cushions ❶, right where the outside of your thighs would normally go. For stability, hold on firmly to the top of the back cushion on the machine. Rotate your femurs to spread your calves apart ❷, but do not push with the outsides of your feet. Once you have rotated as far as possible, hold that position for one or two seconds before letting your feet slowly come back together.

Notes

This exercise is a good way to become aware of where the rotator muscles are and why they are important. Once you have really worked them, you will feel them with every step, and you might feel as though you are walking on eggshells.

Points to Consider

You must begin with a light weight (often with a single plate) so that the muscles in the calves do not work more than the internal rotators. The goal is to rotate the femur as much as possible rather than trying to add weight. Do this exercise slowly and in long sets.

Variations

To warm up on the go or to work out at home without a machine, wrap a resistance band around your feet while kneeling on all fours with your knees on a gym mat 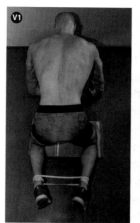. Spread your calves apart without using the outsides of your feet .

Advantages

You will immediately feel a novel sensation in the glutes since this exercise recruits muscles that are seldom used in a dynamic, voluntary way.

Disadvantages

It is very easy to transfer the work to other muscle groups like the calves if you are trying to use a weight that is too heavy.

⚠ Risks

When you begin doing this exercise, you must start with a light weight and do no more than one or two sets since these muscles are fragile and are not used to being worked so intensely.

Do not overdo the range of motion in this exercise. If each calf can rotate 45 degrees, that is already very good.

EXTERNAL HIP ROTATION

Why Should an Athlete Do This Exercise?

This is an isolation exercise that targets all the muscles responsible for externally rotating the femur.

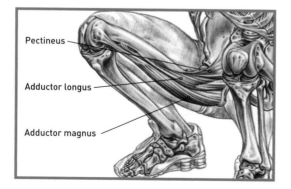

Pectineus

Adductor longus

Adductor magnus

For Which Sports?

This exercise is appropriate for any sport in which you use your legs to move. This movement is especially important in soccer for kicking the ball. In fact, the muscles used to shoot get fatigued faster on the nondominant side. In amateur soccer players who followed the same training protocol, the nondominant leg reached fatigue two or three times faster than the dominant leg.[1] Strength training should strive to reestablish balance between the sides of the body.

To isolate the work to the external rotator muscles, you will use the adductor machine in a different way. Instead of having the moving arms of the machine in front of you, put them behind you. Place your knees on the seat or on the arms of the machine. Hold yourself upright and lean slightly forward so that your thighs form a 90-degree angle with your calves. In this kneeling position, place your feet outside the knee cushions ❶, right where the inner thighs would normally go. For stability, hold on firmly to the top of the back cushion on the machine. Rotate your femurs to squeeze your calves together ❷, but do not pull with your adductors. Hold the position for one or two seconds before letting your feet slowly come apart without trying to reach your maximum rotation.

Advantages

This exercise strengthens muscles that are very difficult to target with strength training.

Disadvantages

It is difficult to do this exercise without a machine.

Points to Consider

You must begin with a light weight (often with only a single plate) so that the adductor muscles do not take over for the external rotators. The goal is to get a good, but not excessive, rotation of the femurs, not to try to add more weight.

⚠ Risks

Only if the range of the arms on the machine can be adjusted, you must be careful not to pull excessively on the rotator muscles during the negative phase of the exercise or as you are getting into the machine. Do not stretch too far when you begin doing this exercise.

EXERCISES FOR GOLF AND SPORTS INVOLVING ROTATION

SEATED PELVIC TILT

Why Should an Athlete Do This Exercise?

✪ To strengthen the muscles that support the lower back when the pelvis is moving (obliques, psoas, quadratus lumborum, and the small deep muscles of the back)

✪ To warm up the low back as a way to prevent lower-back problems and to attempt to minimize any pain that is limiting you before a workout

For Which Sports?

This exercise is for all sports in which the pelvis pivots, such as swimming, golf, and throwing, and sports in which you might want to limit lateral movements, such as running.

Sit on a fitness ball, with your back very straight and your knees bent to 90 degrees. Place your feet flat on the ground with as little weight on them as possible. Transfer your weight to the left glute but keep your torso straight ❶. Pause for one second, and then use your pelvic muscles to transfer your weight to the right glute ❷. Do this exercise in a slow and controlled manner and gradually increase the range as you go.

Keep your upper torso very straight and do not move your shoulders, because the movement should come from the pelvis. To help with this, imagine that you have a book on top of your head and that you must do the exercise without letting the book fall. You can also place your hands on your low back so that you can feel the lower back moving to the side.

Notes

If you are using this as a warm-up before strength training or before playing your sport, you should stop the set before you feel any muscle fatigue. At the end of a workout, you should do as many repetitions as you can until your muscles cannot do any more reps due to fatigue. In both cases, a single set should suffice.

Variations

This exercise requires a learning period with several steps:

✪ To learn to pivot the pelvis without swinging your torso or using your thighs, begin the exercise with your legs wide apart and your hands on the ball to stabilize your torso.

✪ If you feel your glutes contracting, lean your torso slightly forward to reduce the amount they are working.

✪ The closer together your legs are, the harder the exercise is (and the easier it is to swing if you lack strength and control over your muscles).

✪ If you hold on to something stable with your hands, you can lift your legs in the air, which will prevent the thighs from doing any work. But to keep the work

focused on the muscles in the low back, do not assist yourself with your arms.

✪ If you do not have a ball, any soft surface, like a bed or a sofa, will work. The softer the surface is, the bigger the range of motion can be, and this will make the exercise more effective. For people with fragile spines, the exercise can even be done as a warm-up while they are sitting in the car.

Advantages

The goal here is not to walk a tightrope, but rather to target specific muscles that tend to be left behind by classic strengthening exercises. Neglecting these muscles can lead to premature low back fatigue or even back pain.

Disadvantages

Though this exercise might seem simple, it is definitely not. It is much easier to do the exercise poorly or to use the wrong muscles than it is to do it correctly.

⚠ Risks

We recommend that you use a base with the ball so that the ball cannot roll away and cause you to fall.

As a warm-up, this exercise can relieve a small ache in the low back that is preventing you from working out. However, if the pain is too strong, we recommend that you rest instead.

STANDING AB TWIST WITH A RESISTANCE BAND

Why Should an Athlete Do This Exercise?

This exercise prepares and strengthens all the muscles that rotate the torso.

For Which Sports?

This exercise is for all sports in which the torso rotates, in other words, nearly all sports.

Attach a resistance band to a fixed point at elbow height. Stand with the band to your right side and grab it with both hands and your arms bent. Take a step to the side, away from the band **❶**. The distance as well as the resistance supplied by the band determines the total resistance that your muscles will face. It is easy to adjust this resistance by moving closer to or farther away from the attachment point. Spread your legs apart for stability and begin rotating from right to left **❷**. Your right shoulder serves as a pivot point for the band. Do not turn your torso more than 45 degrees. Hold the contracted position for one or two seconds before slowly returning to the starting position. When you have finished the left side, move on to the right side.

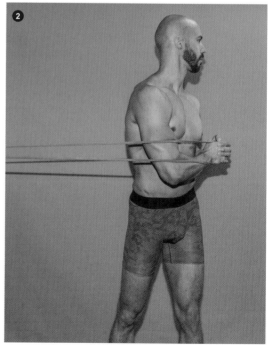

Points to Consider

Begin this first version by keeping your torso perfectly in line with your legs.

Variations

■ WITH SIDE TWISTS

A Once you are very comfortable with the basic version, you can start to lean your torso forward as if you were swinging. Raise the attachment point of the band to the level of your head and pull down on it, first with bent arms and then with straight arms. You can also use a grip similar to what you would use to grasp a club. In this position, get used to keeping the lower back straight. Do not arch or bend your back, even if you are naturally inclined to do so, since this increases your risk of injury. Gradually lifting the attachment point increases the range of this exercise. Later, for a full range of motion, you can also move farther away from the attachment point.

B If you do not have equipment, you can do these rotations on the ground with your arms out to your sides. Bend your legs so that the quadriceps form a 90-degree angle with the torso. From there, lean the knees to the right and then the left.

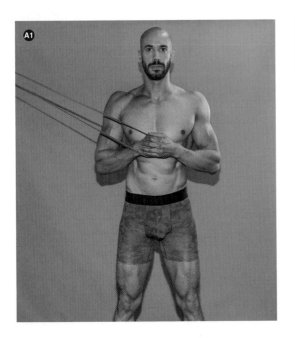

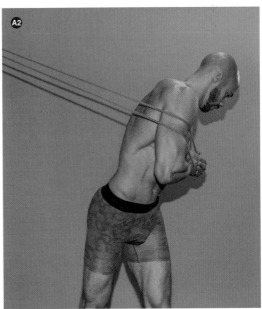

■ ANTIROTATION

C Stand with your arms straight but do not pull on the band. Once you are in position, take small steps to the side to add more resistance to the band. When you feel that the resistance on the band is so great that you can hardly keep your body straight, then stabilize your feet and hold the position for about 10 seconds before returning to the starting position. Repeat by moving the resistance band to the other side of the body. At first, you should keep your arms perpendicular to the ground. To make the exercise harder and work the muscles over their full range of contraction, vary the angle between your arms and the ground. Once you are in position, though, the goal is to keep the band from pulling you out of position. Your torso and arms should not move; only your feet should move.

D Instead of moving your body, gradually straighten your arms in front you to add tension to the band. Then bring your hands next to your torso without moving your waist.

E For leg rotations during lying on the ground, instead of constantly moving your knees, hold them steady once they are halfway to the ground. Hold this position for as long as you can. If that is too easy, straighten the legs to make the work harder. Once you have reached fatigue on one side, switch to the other side.

Notes

At first, rotations should be done slowly, using a small range of motion: You do not want to stretch the torso too much at the beginning. Early gains in strength will rapidly translate to improved performance.

Later, once you have experienced these first benefits (after about a month of regular training), you can modify the exercise to help you continue to make progress in your sport. Instead of increasing resistance, you can gently and gradually increase the range of motion, both during the stretching phase and during the contraction.

Though you should begin by keeping your feet firmly planted on the ground and your legs straight to limit the range of motion, later you can bend your legs and pull your heels off the ground as in golf. End by pushing with the ball of the foot that is on the side where your resistance band is attached; this enables you to recruit the entire muscle chain that works during a swing. The range of motion will then naturally increase all on its own.

However, we do not recommend trying to replicate the full range of motion of your swing. Similarly, though the speed can be slightly increased, we do not recommend doing this exercise explosively.

TIP

Without resistance from the side, there is no point in doing standing twists. Turning frenetically with your golf club on your shoulders does nothing unless you are really starting from scratch. Leaning your torso forward makes the exercise harder, but it still does not precisely target the muscles you use to swing. Doing twists leaning forward really changes the muscle recruitment by involving the low back muscles to a greater degree.

Even a small amount of resistance from a band will always be more effective both for a warm-up and for strengthening the muscles.

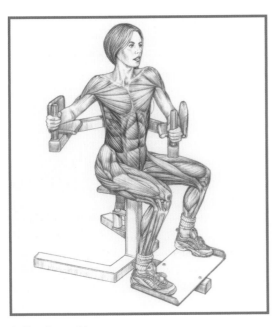

▲ Ab twist machine.

Advantages

Using a resistance band means you can do this exercise anywhere, whether as a warm-up on the go or working out at home. Strengthening the obliques helps prevent very painful tears in these muscles, which are common in sports involving rotation.

Disadvantages

Ab twist machines are available. Even though they are high tech, we believe they are less effective than a simple resistance band because a band lets you work in different positions that are closer to what you experience in your sport.

⚠ Risks

You should not do any kind of twisting exercise if you have back pain or you feel as though your back is compressed. In this case, try seated pelvic tilt exercises (see p. 100) instead, which are much gentler. Similarly, it is best to avoid strength training exercises that involve twisting on the days when you have already played your sport.

PLANK

Why Should an Athlete Do This Exercise?

This is a static exercise that works the entire abdominal area.

Lie facedown on the ground and then lift yourself onto your elbows and the tips of your feet. Keep your body as straight as possible and hold this static position for at least 15 seconds.

TIP
A gym mat, or at least a towel, can help prevent discomfort in your forearms.

For Which Sports?

Plank is good for practically all sports that require good abdominal and lumbar support. For example, if you are a runner, good abdominal support allows you to maintain good posture for longer, which means less pressure on your knees (especially the cruciate ligaments) during sprints in which you are constantly changing direction.[1]

For team sports with a ball, you have to run in all directions, stop suddenly, jump, throw, and withstand varying degrees of impact with your opponents. It is better for you if you can remain on your feet due to proper stability and absorb these impacts without losing your balance.

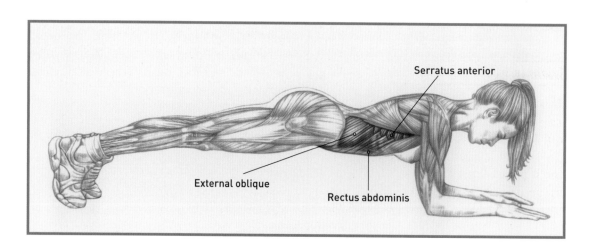

Serratus anterior

External oblique

Rectus abdominis

Variations

A To make the exercise harder, have a partner put a weight plate on your glutes or sit on your butt. Be careful not to arch your back.

B Do the same exercise in the side position to work the obliques. This is an anti-rotation variation that can be used by people whose backs are too fragile to do twists. If this version is too hard at first, you can place your free hand on the ground in front of you for more support.

Advantages

This stability exercise does not require any equipment and can be done very quickly at home. It will quickly increase the power of your swing all while protecting your back since it strengthens muscles that are not often used in daily life and that are naturally very weak.

Disadvantages

Past a certain point, static work is not as effective as dynamic work.

⚠ Risks

Arching the back makes the exercise easier; however, it can cause pinching of the discs.

Even though holding your breath makes the exercise easier, you should not do it. If you have a hard time breathing in this position, you can exhale using small breaths.

SHOULD THE CORE MUSCLES HAVE ENDURANCE, BE EXPLOSIVE, OR BE STRONG?

Although in some sports you need to work on strength and explosiveness in the core muscles (in golf or in throwing sports), in other sports it is better to work on endurance. For example, poor endurance in the core muscles is an important risk factor for low back problems in rowers.[2] Running with weak core muscles increases the pressure on the spine and also the risk for back pain.[3] The longer the distance you run, the more you need to work on core muscle endurance by holding plank for an extended period of time.

WRIST CURL

Why Should an Athlete Do This Exercise?

○ This exercise strengthens the forearms.

○ This exercise protects the wrists, elbows, and forearms from various injuries. In fact, the muscles of the superficial and middle layers of the wrist flexors also help to stabilize the elbow in sports that involve throwing.[4]

For Which Sports?

This exercise is for all sports in which you need to grip strongly or strike with your hands.

Sit down and grab a bar or two dumbbells in a supinated grip (thumbs toward the outside). Place your forearms on your thighs or on a bench; the hands should hang free ❶. Using your forearms, lift your wrists as high as possible ❷. Hold the contracted position for one second before slowly lowering your wrists.

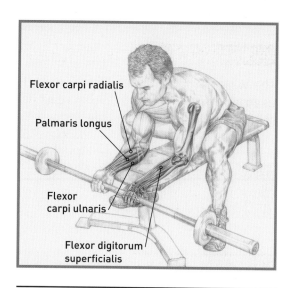

Flexor carpi radialis

Palmaris longus

Flexor carpi ulnaris

Flexor digitorum superficialis

Notes

Bending your arms makes you stronger in this exercise.

Variation

If you do not have equipment or you just want to warm up on the go, you can use a resistance band. Do the same movement that you would do if you had dumbbells (❶ and ❷).

Advantages

This is a simple exercise that can help you avoid debilitating forearm problems.

⚠ Risks

The wrists are fragile joints, yet they are used a lot. Be careful not to overdo the range of motion during this exercise.

Disadvantages

We do not recommend doing this exercise in isolation. Each set of wrist curls should ideally be followed by a set of wrist extensions to balance the strength at the heart of the forearms (see Finger Extension on p. 129).

MYOFASCIAL MASSAGE FOR THE FOREARMS

Why Should an Athlete Do This Massage?

✪ To accelerate recovery
✪ To decrease the pain threshold in a muscle zone that is used often and can be very sensitive

For Which Sports?

This is for all sports that involve the hands.

Kneel on the ground with a massage roller in front of you. Place one forearm on the roller and move back and forth by moving the roller and your forearm. Roll for 1 minute as you rotate the hand so that you can massage the flexors and extensors. Once you have finished massaging one arm, do the other arm.

After a few sessions, you can use your free hand to press on the forearm being massaged to increase the intensity of the massage.

TIP

If one of your forearms cannot tolerate massage or pressure, you can massage the other arm, even if it does not hurt. This will still help relieve pain on the other side.

Variation

If you do not have a roller, you can use a ball that is somewhat firm to do the massage.

Notes

You have to work on the painful areas. The goal is not to make the pain worse, but rather to increase mobility in the different layers that make up the fascia.

Advantages

Myofascial massage is very effective. The forearms are easy to access, so take advantage and massage yourself!

Disadvantages

People usually think about massage once they are already in pain. But massages are just as effective if they are done preventively.

⚠ Risks

One part of the benefits of these massages is that they mask pain, which can be a good thing. When you feel less pain, you can get a higher-quality workout.[5,6] But do not forget that even if you are not feeling as much pain, the injury is still there.

EXERCISES FOR SWIMMING AND NAUTICAL SPORTS

PULL-UP

Why Should an Athlete Do This Exercise?

This exercise will add muscle to the back as well as the back of the shoulders, the biceps, a part of the triceps, and the forearms.

For Which Sports?

This is for all sports, and especially aquatic sports that require intense use of the arms.

Grab the pull-up bar with a pronated grip (thumbs facing each other). Your hands should be about shoulder-width apart. Lift your legs behind you so that your calves form a 90-degree angle with your thighs. Pull yourself up using the strength of your back and arms until your forehead reaches the bar. If you can, lift your chin to the bar before lowering yourself down slowly.

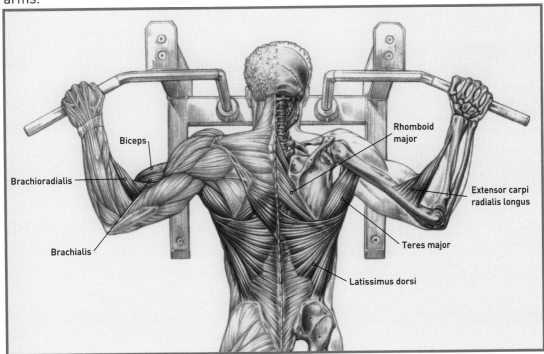

Variations

A If a pull-up is too hard, rest your feet on a chair or a bench to support some of your weight and then do the exercise.

B If you are not strong enough to lift yourself, you can use machines that will provide less resistance.

Advantages

Pull-ups work a very important part of the torso muscles effectively without putting tension on the low back.

Disadvantages

Not everyone can do pull-ups. In this case, you should try some of the easier variations described above.

⚠ Risks

Avoid straightening your arms completely at the bottom of the exercise, because this puts your shoulders and biceps in a position that could lead to injuries.

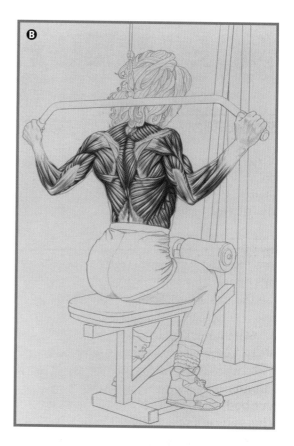

ROW

Why Should an Athlete Do This Exercise?

Rowing works the entire back and the backs of the shoulders, as well as the biceps, forearms, and the long head of the triceps.

For Which Sports?

This exercise is for all sports in which you use the arms intensely.

Lean forward so that your torso forms a 90- to 120-degree angle with the ground. Grab two dumbbells using a neutral grip (thumbs forward) **. Pull your arms along your body while bending them so that you bring your elbows as high as possible and your shoulder blades as close together as possible** ❷ **before lowering the weights.**

TIP

Lying on a bench inclined to 35 degrees will support your spine better.

Variations

Ⓐ You can pull your arms either at the same time, as in the butterfly, or asynchronously, to develop your crawl stroke, for example.

Ⓑ You can also row with a single dumbbell, using one arm at a time.

Ⓒ To warm up on the go or to train at home, use a resistance band instead of dumbbells. Hold the band under your feet and hold the other part in your hands (pronated grip). Pull with your back to bring your hands to your torso. You can do this while standing or while sitting.

Ⓓ Do the exercise with a bar. This variation is good for athletes who need to pull both arms at the same time, for example, when rowing.

Advantages

Rows target the muscles in the middle of the back better than pull-ups do, all while being less risky for the shoulders.

Disadvantages

Though rows are great for certain aquatic sports like rowing, kayaking, or surfing, they are not as well suited for swimming as pull-ups are since you are not lifting your arms into the air.

⚠ Risks

Rows can aggravate a backache.

STRAIGHT-ARM PULL-DOWN

Why Should an Athlete Do This Exercise?

This exercise strengthens the muscles that bring the arms to the body, that is, the latissimus dorsi, the pectoral muscles, and the triceps. The latissimus dorsi works synergistically with the long head of the triceps to bring the arms toward the torso.

For Which Sports?

Pull-downs are good for practically all sports that involve the arms.

Stand in front of a high pulley and grab the small bar with a pronated grip (thumbs facing each other). Keeping the arms straight, bring your hands to the upper quadriceps before returning to the starting position.

Variations

Ⓐ Instead of a bar, you can use two handles (if you have an opposing pulley) or two resistance bands attached to a fixed point at waist height.
Ⓑ Pull with both arms at the same time to work on the butterfly stroke and pull asynchronously to work on the crawl stroke.

Advantages

If you are not yet strong enough to do pull-ups, use this exercise to get stronger. This exercise is also an excellent way to warm up before participating in your sport.

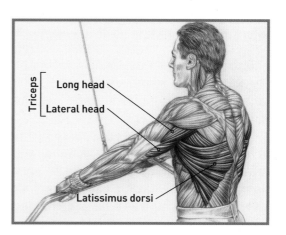

Disadvantages

Some athletes feel this exercise more in the triceps than in the back. If that happens, spread your hands farther apart.

⚠ Risks

Since the pull-down has you lift your arms above your head, it can aggravate a shoulder injury. To avoid this, reduce the range of motion by lowering the pulley and not raising your arms so high.

BENT-OVER LATERAL RAISE

Why Should an Athlete Do This Exercise?

This exercise isolates the backs of the shoulders, the trapezius muscles, the latissimus dorsi, the lower back, and the long head of the triceps.

Lean forward so that your torso forms a 90-degree angle with the ground, and grab two dumbbells (the backs of your hands should be facing each other) ❶. Lift the arms as high as possible, making a Y shape with the body ❷ before lowering back down.

For Which Sports?

This exercise is for all sports that require great strength in the back as well as effective protection from shoulder injury.

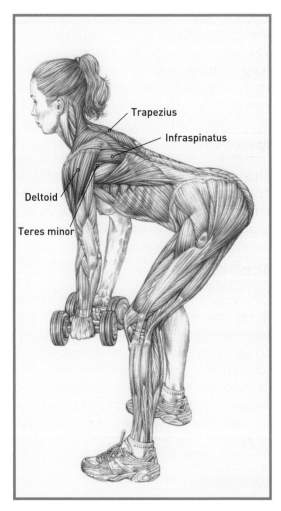

Variation

If you do not have dumbbells, or you want to warm up on the go or train at home, you can use a resistance band. Stand up and hold one end of the band in each hand (pronated grip), with your hands about eight inches apart . Spread your arms as far apart as possible to stretch the band  and then return to the starting position. The advantage—and the disadvantage—of the standing position is that it spares the low back but does not work the muscles in the low back. However, you can always do the exercise while leaning forward or while seated, depending upon how you use these muscles in your sport.

Advantages

This exercise works muscles that are neglected but that are nevertheless very important, not only for performance but also to prevent shoulder injuries.

Disadvantages

Lifting both arms at the same time reproduces the movement found in the butterfly stroke, but not in the crawl stroke. To strengthen your muscles specifically for that stroke, you will need to do this exercise while lifting the arms asynchronously.

⚠ Risks

The bent-over position can create tension in the low back. Force yourself to keep your back very straight.

TIP

Lying on a bench inclined to 35 degrees will support your spine better.

LATERAL RAISE

Why Should an Athlete Do This Exercise?

This exercise strengthens the shoulders by working muscles that are not often used.

For Which Sports?

This exercise is for all sports in which you lift the arms up in the air.

Stand up and grab two dumbbells using a neutral grip (thumbs facing forward). Begin with the weights placed on the outside of the thighs ❶. Lift the arms to the side, as straight as possible, keeping the arms in line with the body ❷.

Notes

Bending your arms more makes the exercise easier, but the lateral part of the deltoid works less as a result.

Advantages

This exercise works muscles that you do not typically have the opportunity to strengthen on a daily basis.

Disadvantages

If you have shoulder pain, do not lift your arms too high.

Variations

Ⓐ If your natural flexibility permits, instead of stopping your arms when they are parallel to the ground, bring them above your head. This high version is great for swimmers.
Ⓑ Instead of lifting your arms to the side, lift them in front of you to do front raises. These are very useful for throwing sports like petanque or bowling.

⚠ Risks

Jerking with your torso may allow you to lift heavier weights, but it could cause pinching in your lumbar spine.

SHOULDER ROTATION WITH A RESISTANCE BAND

Why Should an Athlete Do This Exercise?

Shoulder rotations are an isolation exercise that targets the muscles in the rotator cuff. Beyond just strengthening these muscles, shoulder rotations are especially good for warming up your muscles correctly before a workout.

For Which Sports?

Shoulder rotations are for all sports that require shoulder movement.

■ INTERNAL ROTATIONS

Stand with your arms near your sides while holding a long, but weak, resistance band behind your back in both hands in a supinated grip (pinky fingers facing each other). Next, spread your arms apart to stretch the band ❶. Without releasing any tension, rotate your wrists and shoulders to bring your thumbs to the inside ❷. The band will roll around the pinky fingers. Once your thumbs are facing each other, return to the starting position and keep repeating the exercise.

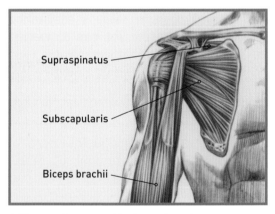

▲ The muscles targeted by internal rotations.

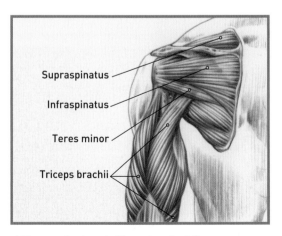

▲ The muscles targeted by external rotations.

■ EXTERNAL ROTATIONS

Stand with your arms near your sides while holding a resistance band behind your back in both hands in a pronated grip (thumbs facing each other). Next, spread your arms apart to stretch the band ❶. Without releasing any tension, rotate your shoulders to bring your thumbs to the outside ❷. The band will roll around the thumbs. Once your thumbs are facing away from each other, return to the star-ting position and keep repeating the exercise.

TIP

When doing external rotations, squeeze the shoulder blades tightly together during the contraction phase of the exercise.

Points to Consider

You can adjust the resistance by pulling more or less on the resistance band.

Do this exercise in long sets of 30 to 50 repetitions using the largest range of motion possible without forcing your shoulders.

Notes

These rotations must come from the shoulders and not the wrists.

Advantages

It is easy always to carry a resistance band with you so that you can do warm-up exercises, both before playing your sport and before strength training.

Disadvantages

It is hard to measure and therefore to reproduce the exact amount of resistance provided by a band.

⚠ Risks

If you have shoulder pain, the rotated position where the hands are low can irritate the long head of the biceps. In this case, try the version with the hand in the air described in the following exercise.

EXTERNAL ARM ROTATION

Why Should an Athlete Do This Exercise?

This exercise strengthens the external rotator muscles of the shoulder.

For Which Sports?

This exercise is for all sports that require shoulder movement, especially when you also have to lift the arms above the head.

Sit on the ground or on a bench in front of an adjustable pulley. Turn your side to the machine and grab the handle (set at a level that is near the middle of your body). Place your right elbow on your knee or on a bench to form a 90-degree angle with the forearm ❶. Lift your hand in the air until your forearm is perpendicular to the ground ❷. Return to the starting position without letting the forearm go any lower than parallel to the ground.

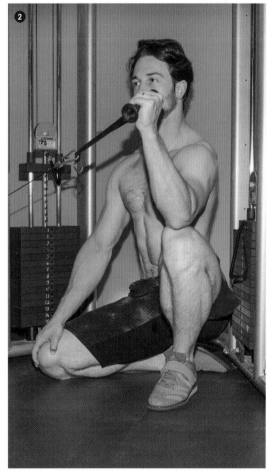

Points to Consider

Try to find the angle between the arm and the body that is the most natural for you. This angle is not the same for everyone.

Notes

Do not wait until you experience shoulder pain to start worrying about your rotator cuff.

Variations

If you do not have a pulley and you want to warm up on the go or train at home, you can use a resistance band attached at your side near the middle of your body . You should be kneeling or seated on the ground or on a bench. Rest your elbow on your thigh or a bench to do the exercise .

Advantages

This is an excellent warm-up and strengthening exercise for all sports that involve shoulder movement.

Disadvantages

This exercise can easily be done with a dumbbell, but that version is more traumatic and therefore riskier for the shoulder. The goal of strength training is to strengthen the body, not to damage it.

⚠ Risks

Do not let the weight pull your hand too low toward the ground during the stretching phase. You must maintain perfect control throughout the exercise.

PULLEY SHOULDER ROTATION

Why Should an Athlete Do This Exercise?

This exercise provides another angle of attack to strengthen the infraspinatus muscle.

For Which Sports?

This exercise is for all sports that require shoulder movement.

■ **WITH AN ADJUSTABLE PULLEY**
Stand with your feet slightly apart and bend your left arm to 90 degrees while keeping the inner part of your biceps against your torso. Use your left hand to grab the handle, which should be placed at midlevel height on your right side ❶. Use a neutral grip (thumb facing up). Rotate your forearm as if you were hitchhiking. Go as far to the left as possible ❷. Hold the contracted position for one second before bringing your forearm back to the right.

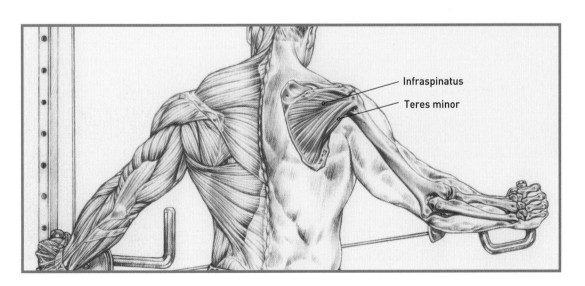

Infraspinatus

Teres minor

Variation

If you do not have a pulley and you want to warm up on the go or train at home, grab a resistance band that you have attached at about waist height **Ⓥ**.

■ **LYING ON A BENCH WITH DUMBBELLS**
Lie on your belly on a bench with your arms out to the side and bent at the elbows. Hold a small dumbbell in each hand using a pronated grip (thumbs facing each other) ❶. Lift the weights without straightening the arms until your forearms are parallel to the ground ❷. Hold the contraction for at least one second before lowering the weights.

Advantages

Keeping your arms near your sides allows you to continue training even if you have some irritation in the supraspinatus.

Disadvantages

This exercise is often done with dumbbells while standing up. Unfortunately, this is completely ineffective because the resistance needs to come from the side and not from the top to the bottom.

⚠ Risks

If your biceps tendon is irritated, bring your elbows forward instead of keeping them exactly to the side. This softens the biceps tendon and will reduce its rubbing on the bone.

EXERCISES FOR RACQUET AND THROWING SPORTS

RING FLY, SUSPENDED PUSH-UP, AND DIP USING RINGS OR SUSPENSION STRAPS

Why Should an Athlete Do This Exercise?

With simple rings or suspension straps, you can do three types of movements:

✪ Ring flys to strengthen the pectoral muscles and the front part of the shoulders

✪ Suspended push-ups or presses, which target the pectoral muscles, the shoulders (especially the front), and the triceps

✪ Dips, which target the pectoral muscles, a little bit of the front of the shoulders, and the triceps

For Which Sports?

These exercises are for all sports in which you project your arms in front of your body or over your head.

■ RING FLY

Stand up and grab the two handles. Support yourself on the straps as you place your feet on a bench behind you. Your arms should be straight, and your body should be at about a 135-degree angle to the floor ❶. Bend your arms slightly and spread them to the side so that they are both in the same line ❷. Hold this position with your arms out to the side for one second; then, lift your torso up using your pectoral muscles. Once your hands are close together, hold the contracted position for one second before moving the handles apart once again.

■ SUSPENDED PUSH-UP

Stand up and grab the two handles. Support yourself on the straps as you place your feet on a bench behind you. Your arms should be straight with your thumbs facing each other, and your body should be at about a 135-degree angle to the floor ❶.

Lower your torso as you bend your elbows, just as in a push-up ❷. Hold the low position for one second before lifting your torso up using your pectoral and triceps muscles. Once your arms are almost straight, lower back down.

■ DIP

Stand up and grab the two handles. Straighten your arms as you support yourself on the straps and lift your calves ❶. Lower your torso by bending at the

elbows to bring your hands more or less to your lower chest ❷. Push on your arms to lift your body back up. Once your arms are almost straight, lower back down.

Points to Consider

Unlike a chest fly with dumbbells, there is no loss of tension at the top of the movement with the ring fly. This is an enormous advantage for javelin or disc throwers, for example.

Notes

At the beginning, you will tremble like a leaf, especially in the straight-arm positions, because you lack muscle coordination. After that, you will make fast progress, and, in a few sessions, the shakiness will be nothing more than a bad memory.

The more unstable you are, the more the work spreads around the whole body. This creates better muscle activation, which is closer to what you need when playing sports.

Variations

These three exercises can be done with weights or even with machines. The primary advantage of suspended straps is that since your torso is not blocked by a bench, the movements are closer to the kinds of movements used in many sports.

Advantages

These straps are very practical for training at home with little equipment. For a modest price, they can replace a great deal of bulky training equipment. You can even make them yourself out of rope, carabiners, and two handles. However, you will need two attachment points that are very strong, like the upper part of a squat cage, for example.

Disadvantages

Keep in mind that when you are first starting out, an exercise in an unstable environment is more arduous than the same exercise done in a stable environment.

⚠ Risks

When doing ring flys or suspended push-ups, the stretch could be risky if your muscles are weak. To avoid any accidents, adjust the size of the straps so that you are very close to the ground. This way, in case you fall, you will not dislocate your shoulder or tear a pectoral muscle because the floor will immediately stop your torso. For dips, we recommend that you ensure your feet can always touch the ground.

Why Should an Athlete Do This Exercise?

This exercise strengthens the internal rotator muscles of the shoulder.

For Which Sports?

This exercise is for all sports that require you to pull the arm backward to throw (e.g., handball, baseball, javelin) and is appropriate if you want to get stronger in arm wrestling.

Points to Consider

Try to find the angle between the arm and the body that is the most natural for you. This angle is not the same for everyone.

Sit in front of an adjustable pulley. Turn your side to the machine and grab the handle (set at a level that is near the middle of your body). Place your elbow on your knee or on a bench to form a 90-degree angle with the forearm ❶. Lower your hand as if you were arm wrestling and bring your forearm parallel to the ground ❷. Return to the starting position without bringing your hand past the point where it is perpendicular to the ground.

⚠ Risks

Do not let the weight pull your hand too far backward as you bring the arm up. You must maintain perfect control throughout the exercise.

Variations

If you do not have a pulley and you want to warm up on the go or train at home, you can use a resistance band attached to the side of you. You should be kneeling or seated on the ground behind a bench or an object on which you can rest your elbow (V1 and V2).

Advantages

This is an excellent exercise to use to warm up or to increase strength, and it can be used for all sports involving shoulder movement.

Disadvantages

Ideally, you should do this exercise while standing up with your arms out to your sides and bent to 90 degrees at the elbow. However, when you first begin, your arms will not stay in place without support, which deprives the rotator muscles of proper stimulation. It is better to begin with the version we have described so that you can master the muscle contraction, even if it does not exactly match what happens in your sport.

FINGER EXTENSION

Why Should an Athlete Do This Exercise?

This is a specific warm-up and strengthening exercise for the wrist and finger extensor muscles.

■ ON A BENCH
Sit on a bench, a bed, or another surface. and support yourself with straight arms on the backs of your hands against the surface of the bench ❶. Use your fingers to lift your arms just as you would lift yourself up onto the tips of your toes ❷. Once you are almost at the end of your fingers, drop back down onto the backs of your hands.

For Which Sports?

This is for all sports that use a lot of hand strength.

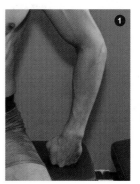 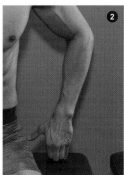

Notes

Use this exercise as a warm-up at the beginning of training, both before your sport and before any upper-body strength training.

■ **WITH A FINGER REHABILITATION BAND**
Place the rehab band around your fingers ❶. Straighten the working arm fully so that you will be stronger. In fact, the more your elbow bends, the weaker your extensor muscles are. Open your hand as much as possible ❷. Hold this contracted position, with an open hand, for at least one second before closing your fingers, and then repeat the exercise.

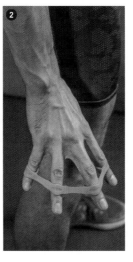

Notes

Rehab bands, which cost only a few dollars, are very beneficial for all athletes who have to use their hands.

Advantages

These simple exercises can strengthen muscles in the forearms that are often very neglected.

Disadvantages

You can easily open your hand even if the pinky is providing minimal effort. This is not the best way to strengthen this finger even though it is the weakest of all the fingers. Begin the set by concentrating on working the pinky, ensuring that it opens and closes over a good range of motion. When it gets tired, you can let the other fingers, which are stronger, take over some of the work.

⚠ Risks

The small muscles of the hand are not accustomed to working intensely. Begin this exercise by using a small amount of resistance; you can increase this gradually as you go.

WRIST EXTENSION

Why Should an Athlete Do This Exercise?

✪ To strengthen the forearms
✪ To protect the wrists, elbows, and forearms from injury

For Which Sports?

This is for all sports in which you need to grip something firmly or strike with your hands.

Points to Consider

The straighter your arms are, the stronger you will be during this exercise.

Sit down and grab a bar or two dumbbells in a pronated grip (thumbs facing each other). Place your forearms on your thighs or on a bench and let your hands hang free ❶. Use your forearms to lift your wrists as high as possible ❷. Hold the contraction for one second before slowly lowering your wrists.

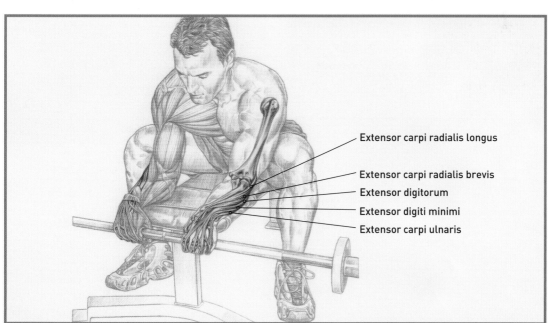

Extensor carpi radialis longus

Extensor carpi radialis brevis

Extensor digitorum

Extensor digiti minimi

Extensor carpi ulnaris

Variations

Ⓐ If you do not have dumbbells and you want to warm up on the go or to train at home, use a resistance band held under your feet.

Ⓑ If you do not have a band, you can do hand extensions by bending the wrists in the seated position described in the exercise Finger Extension (see p. 129).

Advantages

The movements in this exercise can help you avoid injuries that can be debilitating for an athlete.

Disadvantages

Each set of wrist extensions should ideally be followed by a series of forearm flexion exercises to balance out the strength in the forearm (see Wrist Curl on p. 108). Do not forget to do myofascial massages for the forearms (see p. 109) to accelerate recovery between workouts.

⚠ Risks

Do not push your wrist too far into the bench, especially when your muscles are cold, because you do not want to cause an injury.

REVERSE CURL

Why Should an Athlete Do This Exercise?

✪ To strengthen the forearms and arms
✪ To prevent injuries, especially tennis elbow

Grab a dumbbell in each hand with your arms at the sides of your body ❶. Use a semipronated grip (thumbs almost facing each other but still turned a bit toward the ceiling) and bend your arms, keeping your thumbs a little bit higher than your fingers. Bring the dumbbells as high as you can without lifting your elbows (the elbows should stay glued to the torso throughout the exercise) ❷. Once your hands are lifted as high as possible, lower back down to the starting position.

For Which Sports?

This exercise is for all sports involving the hands and arms.

Notes

You can do this exercise with both hands at the same time or asynchronously, with one hand at a time.

Variations

Ⓐ You can use a resistance band, which is less traumatic for the wrists than dumbbells. If you use a band, you can do the exercise while standing or while lying down. The latter position is especially good if you have back pain.
Ⓑ Often, people use a long, straight bar to do this exercise, but this can be more traumatic for the wrists than using dumbbells.

Advantages

Unlike wrist extensions, this exercise does not mobilize the wrists, so it is less likely to cause overuse injuries.

Disadvantages

This is a strengthening exercise and should not be used to warm up before your sporting activity.

⚠ Risks

If you experience any tension in your wrists, then you should use straps to alleviate the pressure in this zone.

HIP ADDUCTION

Why Should an Athlete Do This Exercise?

This exercise strengthens the adductors so as to avoid strains or tears.

For Which Sports?

This exercise is for all sports in which you use your legs to move, especially those in which you move laterally.

Sit in the machine and place your legs on the arms ❶. Slowly squeeze your thighs as close together as possible ❷. Hold the contracted position for one second before returning to the starting position, and then repeat.

Points to Consider

In the starting position, be careful not to stretch your adductors too far.

Notes

Some machines allow you to work with straight legs, and others let you work with bent legs.

Variation

If you do not have a machine and you want to warm up on the go or train at home, you can sit in the tailor position and place your elbows between your knees. Clasp your hands together and bend your arms to 90 degrees to provide resistance **V1**. Squeeze your legs together as much as you can while resisting with your arms **V2**.

Advantages

This exercise helps to strengthen muscles that are vulnerable because they are naturally weak.

Disadvantages

Be careful not to let the machine force your legs too far apart. Maintain perfect control over the range of motion.

⚠ Risks

Do not go beyond your natural range of motion since this could harm your hip joint.

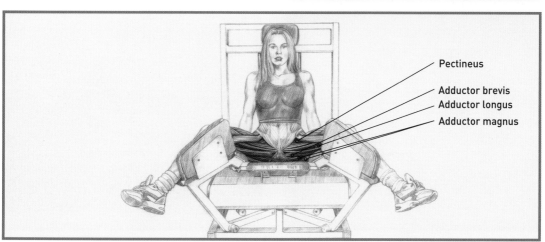

Pectineus

Adductor brevis
Adductor longus
Adductor magnus

EXERCISES FOR CYCLING AND ROAD SPORTS

BELT SQUAT

Why Should an Athlete Do This Exercise?

This basic exercise works the entire thigh and the glutes.

For Which Sports?

This exercise is for all sports in which you pedal, run, jump, or push with your thighs or in which you need excellent stability.

Place the belt around your waist and stand with your feet shoulder-width apart ❶. Release the safety mechanisms and squat by bending your knees ❷. Stand back up and repeat the exercise.

TIP

In addition to the weight, you can add resistance bands to make the exercise more dynamic, especially during the negative phase.

Variations

Ⓐ Keeping your back as straight as possible will focus the work on the quadriceps.

Ⓑ Leaning the torso very far forward will focus the work on the hamstrings and glutes but less on the quadriceps, which can reduce tension in your knees.

Ⓒ The wider apart you place your feet, the more the adductors work, which is important for preventing tears in these muscles, particularly in sports that require lateral movement.

Ⓓ To work the entire thigh in a single exercise, begin with your back straight. As you move through the set, lean your torso forward a little more with each repetition so that your hamstrings and glutes can compensate for fatigue in the quadriceps.

Advantages

The belt squat does not compress the spine the way the classic squat exercise with a bar on the shoulders does. This means you can lean forward without putting your low back at risk.

Pushing the glutes backward puts less pressure on the knees, which is less traumatic for them.

Disadvantages

The two thighs work symmetrically, which is not what happens when you are running.

Though the muscles that propel the leg backward are perfectly stimulated, those that lift the knee are not. You will need to strengthen them using specific exercises (see Exercises for Running Sports on p. 66).

⚠ Risks

Be sure you are in the correct position in the machine right from the start; otherwise the belt could pull you forward and make you fall. Ideally, you should ensure that your feet are in the correct position during your warm-up sets.

BACK EXTENSION ON AN INCLINE BENCH

Why Should an Athlete Do This Exercise?

This exercise strengthens the low back muscles, the glutes, and the hamstrings.

For Which Sports?

This exercise is for all sports that create tension in the spine and require powerful spinal muscles, both to transmit force from the lower body to the upper body and to prevent injuries.

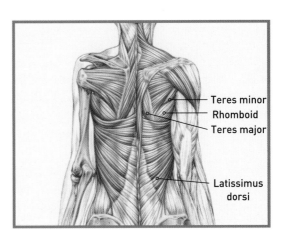

Teres minor
Rhomboid
Teres major

Latissimus dorsi

■ ON A 45-DEGREE BENCH

Lie facedown on the bench with your ankles hooked under the cushions. Relax your torso so that it is perpendicular to the ground. Use your lower-back muscles to lift your torso until it forms a 45-degree angle with the ground before lowering back down.

■ ON A STRAIGHT BENCH

To make the exercise harder, use a bench that is parallel to the ground instead of a bench set at 45 degrees ❶. Lift the torso so that it is more or less parallel to the ground ❷. Hold this position for one or two seconds before lowering back down.

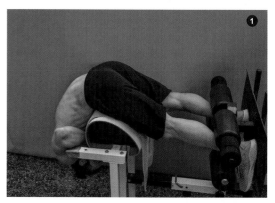

Points to Consider

Sometimes people say that you should not lift the torso past where it is parallel to the ground. However, unless you have back pain or are doing the exercise forcefully, going past parallel should not be an issue. The most interesting part of the contraction happens just above parallel; it is called hyperextension. You should avoid hyperextension while standing up, but when you are lying down, gravity is not pressing on the nuclei of your discs. You do not have to bend your back in two to get your torso perpendicular to the ground either; you will naturally feel the moment when the lumbar muscles cannot lengthen any more.

Notes

It is easier to train on a 45-degree bench because that angle provides less resistance for you to overcome. If you choose to work on a straight bench, try to use a newer one that allows you also to push with your calves.

Variations

No matter which bench you use, there are two techniques for back extensions:

Ⓐ Lower the thigh support as much as possible, so it is close to the foot support. The movement is initiated at the pelvis. It is especially driven by the back of the thighs and the glutes and is helped along by the sacrolumbar muscles. The latter muscles remain in an isometric contraction, which causes a burn and might give the impression that they are doing all the work. This kind of isometric contraction is found in many sports in which the lumbar muscles just support the spine without assisting in movement (cycling, riding motorcycles, skiing).

Ⓑ Raise the thigh support as high as possible, so it is far from the foot support. This movement works the low back dynamically. Your spine unrolls and rolls up the back like a snail. The movement starts from the lower spine, and the spine rolls up as you come up. This is the kind of contraction seen in sports where you have to pick someone or something up, such as an opponent during a fight, in American football, or in rugby.

Ⓒ To warm up on the go or to train at home, you can use a resistance band attached to a low fixed point in front of you to create a hybrid movement between a deadlift and a back extension.

Advantages

Even if you do not do this exercise, simply letting your back hang down, perpendicular to the ground, effectively stretches the spine. You should adopt this regenerative position systematically after each workout along with hanging from a bar.

Disadvantages

It is difficult to add resistance to this exercise without changing the center of gravity and therefore risking transferring the muscle work from the low back muscles to other muscles.

⚠ Risks

Lifting the spine abruptly into hyperextension can be dangerous. Lift up slowly, keeping in mind that this method works the spinal muscles through dynamic and isometric contractions, which is what these muscles were made for.

HYBRID JM PRESS/BENCH PRESS

Why Should an Athlete Do This Exercise?

This basic exercise targets the triceps, the front of the shoulders, and the chest.

For Which Sports?

This exercise is for all sports in which you need to take actions such as these:

✪ Stabilize your torso while pushing on handlebars, as in cycling, motocross, and driving sports
✪ Push an adversary away, as in combat sports, rugby, or American football
✪ Strike an opponent, as in boxing
✪ Bring your arms back to your body, as in swimming or sailing

■ JM PRESS

Lie on a bench or a gym mat on the ground and grab the bar using a medium or narrow grip ❶. Bend your elbows to lower the bar toward the middle of your neck ❷. Adjust how far you lower the bar based on the health of your elbows. To lift the heaviest weight possible, the movement can often be only half of your maximum range of motion. A full range is when the forearms reach the biceps without the shoulders or elbows moving. To go lower, which is always possible, you will notice that movement begins at the shoulders and the elbows get lower instead of remaining pointed up. You have reached the optimal angle between the forearms and arms when the triceps brush the bench or ground. Lift back up and repeat.

Points to Consider

At first glance, the JM press resembles a lying-down triceps extension. But instead of bringing the bar toward the forehead or behind the head, you control your elbows by lowering your hands only toward the neck, using a partial range of motion.

■ BENCH PRESS

From the same starting position used in the JM press **❶**, bring the bar to your lower chest **❷**. If you are lying on the ground, your elbows will reach their lowest point faster than if you are lying on a bench.

Points to Consider

It is not necessarily useful to lower the bar all the way to the chest, especially if you have long forearms.

■ HYBRID JM PRESS/BENCH PRESS

What is unique about this exercise is that you bring the bar to a point between the neck and the lower chest, depending on what is comfortable for the length of your forearms and what your elbows can tolerate. Another way to use this hybrid version is to begin with a JM press. Once you reach failure, instead of putting the bar down, start doing bench presses.

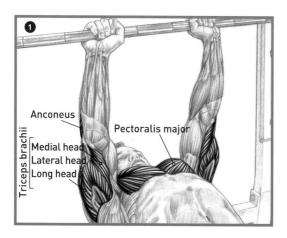

Notes

Adjust the width between your arms based on the arm width you use most often in your sport. For example, a cyclist's grip should be similar to the width of the handlebars (narrower for road cycling and wider for all-terrain).

In boxing, you rarely strike toward the outside with your elbows far from the body; thus, your grip should be narrow, just a bit outside your torso.

Variations

A Using an EZ bar puts less stress on the wrists than using free weights. You can also use two dumbbells or a power rack.

B To warm up on the go or to train at home, attach a strong resistance band to a point behind you at about waist height. Move toward the band and, while standing, push the band forward at neck height.

C You can also push the band forward at chest height.

Advantages

This is a complete exercise for the torso for sports that require a great deal of pushing power.

Disadvantages

The elbows are fragile joints. Even though this exercise is one of the least traumatic for the elbows, you should still avoid using a larger range of motion if you have any elbow pain.

⚠ Risks

Using a "false grip" (thumb on the same side as the fingers) is popular in this type of exercise; however, there is always a risk of losing your grip on the bar if you hold it this way.

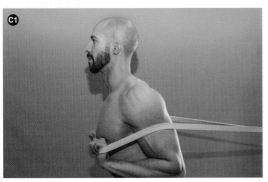

EXERCISES FOR COMBAT SPORTS

BRIDGE (HIP THRUST)

Why Should an Athlete Do This Exercise?

The bridge exercise strengthens numerous muscles, primarily the glutes, the hamstrings, the low back, the quadriceps, and the calves.[1]

Biceps femoris

Gluteus maximus

For Which Sports?

This exercise applies directly to combat sports since it allows you to throw off an opponent easily if you are pinned on the floor. If you are standing, all the muscles targeted by this exercise will help you remain more anchored to the ground with better balance. More generally, bridge exercises are useful in sports in which you use your legs to move (e.g., in running, jumping, leaping, sidestepping).

Starting Position

■ **WITH AN OLYMPIC BAR**
Sit on the ground with straight legs. With your hands, roll a weighted bar (placed near your feet) all the way to your groin. Once the bar is in place, grasp it securely with your hands and do not let go until the weights are touching the ground again. The more you lift your glutes, the greater the chance that the bar could slip toward your abdomen. Do not let this happen.

■ **ON A MACHINE**
Adjust the weight as well as the height of the bench before getting on. Once in place, strap yourself in or lower the cushion to your groin.

▲ Different bridge (hip thrust) machines.

Movement

Bend the knees to 90 degrees by bringing your heels toward your femurs ❶. Use your glutes and push with your feet to lift your abdomen so that your thighs and your torso form a triangle with the ground ❷. The backs of the shoulders and the upper back stay in contact with the ground or the bench to make a lever. Hold the contracted position for one second while squeezing your glutes as much as possible, and then return to the starting position. Repeat the exercise without ever touching your torso to the ground. When you cannot do any more reps, take a short break and lie on the ground before doing a few additional reps.

Points to Consider

The most frequent mistake people make in this exercise is sacrificing some of their range of motion in order to lift heavier. However, only at the end of the set is it better to reduce the range of motion so that you can continue working rather than stopping because you cannot lift your glutes as high as possible.

Notes

✪ More and more machines are now available to do bridges (hip thrusts). They are not any more effective than simply using a bar, but they are more comfortable.

✪ Some machines allow you to rest your back on a bench to increase the range of motion, and this makes the exercise harder.

Variations

Ⓐ Adjust the width of your feet based on your goals:
✪ Narrow feet, close to the glutes, will work the quadriceps more than the hamstrings.
✪ Wide feet, farther away from the glutes, will work the hamstrings more than the quadriceps.
Ⓑ If you do not have a machine, you can use a power rack. This will prevent the bar from moving or rolling.
Ⓒ Without equipment, working on the ground, this exercise can quickly become too easy. It can always still be used as a warm-up. To make it harder, you can do it on one leg. Once you have finished a set on the right leg, move immediately to the left, without resting, to work on your endurance as well as your strength.

Advantages

Bridges (hip thrusts) work the glutes but place less pressure on the lumbar region (this does not mean there is no pressure) than squats or deadlifts. You can maintain a strong contraction in the glutes at the top of the movement, but you lose that in the other two exercises.[1]

Disadvantages

When using weight, this exercise can quickly become very uncomfortable for some people.

⚠ Risks

Ideally, you should use large weight plates so that you can easily slide under the bar. With smaller plates, you could end up pinched under the weighted bar. If you are using heavy weights, be sure that the bar will not crush you in case of a problem during the exercise; the weight plates should always be able to touch the ground.

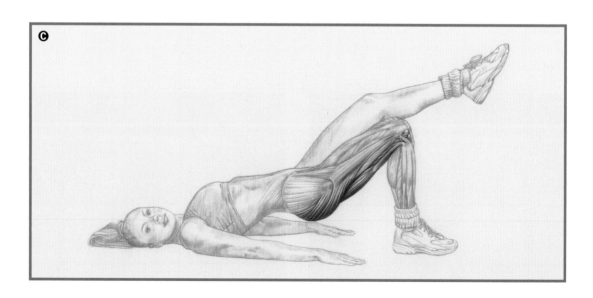

SQUAT WITH A TRAP BAR OR ON A DEADLIFT MACHINE

Why Should an Athlete Do This Exercise?

This is a basic exercise for the entire leg and the back. Since it does not affect the center of gravity as much as a squat with a bar on the shoulders, even a tall athlete can stay relatively straight, which reduces the risk of a low back injury.

For Which Sports?

This exercise is for all sports that require you to move or stabilize yourself with your legs. In combat sports, the better you are at this exercise, the lighter your opponents will seem and the easier it will be to manipulate and immobilize them.

THE DIFFERENCES BETWEEN A SQUAT AND A DEADLIFT

The squat and the deadlift are classic exercises in strength training and are fairly similar, especially in regard to how the thighs move. Nevertheless, studies show that lower-body muscle strength increases more with deadlifts than it does with squats.[2] The deadlift also addresses starting strength more effectively (see Understanding RFD on p. 15), which is better for increasing explosiveness during a confrontation or a standing start sprint.

The primary difference between these two exercises is in how you hold the bar, because this affects the center of gravity. In bar squats, you try to keep the back as straight as possible. In the deadlift, you voluntarily lean forward. But these differences largely disappear when you use a trap bar or a machine, especially with respect to muscle recruitment.[3, 4] Given that you stand up straighter, the activity of the lumbar muscles (and the glutes) is reduced by 27 percent on average. However, quadriceps recruitment increases by 32 percent to 64 percent depending on whether you adopt a squat or a deadlift position. This exercise is more effective for athletes who use their quadriceps a lot for running. Other athletes can lean their torsos slightly forward if they want to recruit the glutes and lumbar muscles more than the quadriceps.

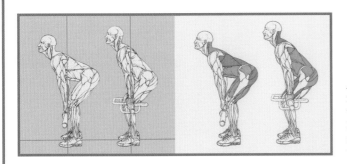

A trap bar helps you keep your torso more upright than a traditional bar, and this spares the back, especially the low back. Additionally, it affects muscle recruitment, shifting the work to the thighs versus the back and the glutes.

■ WITH A TRAP BAR

Place your feet inside the trap bar. Keep your back straight as you crouch down to grab the bar ❶. Use your thighs and back muscles to stand up ❷. Once your legs are straight or semistraight, lower down again and then stand back up.

■ WITH A DEADLIFT MACHINE

Step backward into the machine. Keep your back straight as you crouch down to grab the arms of the machine ❶. Use your thigh and back muscles to stand up ❷. Once your legs are straight or semi-straight, lower down again and then stand back up.

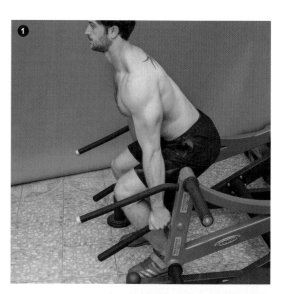

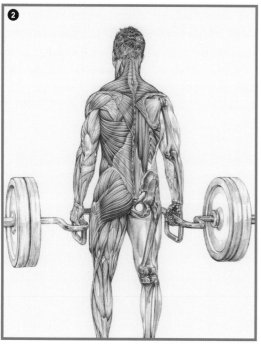

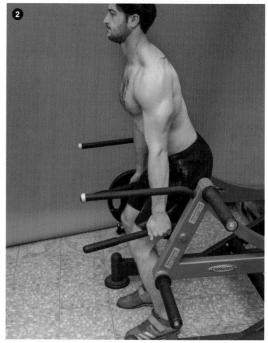

Points to Consider

It is not beneficial to do squats and dead-lifts in the same workout session. The primary interest in using a trap bar or a deadlift machine is to combine the benefits of the squat and the deadlift into a single exercise, which saves a lot of time.

Notes

If you have trouble holding the trap bar or the arms of the machine, do not hesitate to use straps. These will ensure your hands do not tire out before your thighs.

Variation

If you do not have access to a trap bar or a machine, then do the exercise with your arms alongside your body and a dumbbell in each hand.

Advantages

If you use a neutral grip, the risk of biceps tears—which are common in deadlifts using a reverse grip—is greatly reduced.

Disadvantages

You must start from a low position, which is always uncomfortable. However, it does permit you to work on explosiveness if you allow the weight to rest on the ground for several seconds in between reps.

⚠ Risks

Though there is less instability in the lumbar region when you do squats than when you do classic deadlifts, the low back is still under pressure. This decreases, but does not eliminate, the risk of injury.

Why Should an Athlete Do This Exercise?

✪ This exercise has the potential to mobilize all the joints.

✪ It targets all the muscles in the body, especially the front of the shoulder, the chest, the triceps, and the thighs.

For Which Sports?

This exercise is for all contact and throwing sports.

Stand in the machine with one leg in front of you and the other behind you for good stability. Grab the handles. Support yourself on the balls of your feet, with your back very straight, and push on the machine to straighten your arms. Return to the starting position and repeat. You can work both arms together or separately.

Notes

More and more often, jammer arms are being integrated into squat racks. Their advantage over specific machines is in the ability to adjust the grip height, which allows you to alter the ratio of shoulder and chest muscle recruitment.

✪ The higher the arms of the machine are, the more the front parts of the shoulder work.

✪ The lower the arms are, the more the pectoral muscles work.

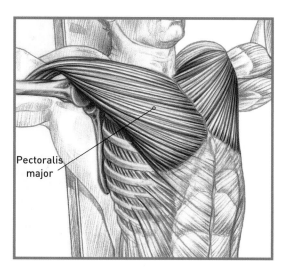

Pectoralis major

Variation

If you do not have a jammer machine, you can reproduce the movement with an Olympic bar. Place one end on the ground and secure it in a corner or in a squat rack.

Advantages

This exercise works the deltoids while minimizing the risk of shoulder damage since you are not lifting the arm all the way in the air, as is often the case in basic shoulder exercises.

Disadvantages

The angle at which you push is not necessarily the same angle you will encounter in your sport. Especially if you play contact sports, try to bend your legs to varying degrees during your sets to change the angle at which the muscles work.

⚠ Risks

As in shoulder presses, you will feel stronger if you arch your back, but this means you will not be working your deltoids to the same degree and will also be risking the integrity of your low back.

COMBO TWIST WITH SIMULTANEOUS PULLING AND PUSHING

Why Should an Athlete Do This Exercise?

This basic exercise targets all the muscles, especially those in the upper body (front of the shoulders, chest, triceps, back, and biceps), and promotes core strength.

For Which Sports?

This exercise is for all contact sports, sports with rotation, and those that require lots of shoulder and arm movement.

Stand in the machine with one leg in front of you and the other behind you for good stability. Grab the handles ❶. Support yourself on the balls of your feet, with your back very straight, and push on the machine to straighten the bent arm while pulling with the other arm and bending it. Repeat ❷.

Points to Consider

At the end of the exercise, you have done only a half set. The full set is complete only after both arms have done the pulling and pushing. To do this, you will need to turn 180 degrees in the machine.

Notes

You can work on strength in the usual way by resting after each half set or even after each complete set. You can also do sets in a circuit to work on both strength and endurance.

Variations

❹ Do this exercise with one arm at a time or both arms at the same time. Working unilaterally means you can focus just on pushing or pulling, depending on what you need in your sport. However, it is better to work on both aspects to reduce the all too frequent risk of a strength imbalance between the front and back of the shoulders.

❺ Rotate your torso during the exercise to increase the range of motion.

C Do the exercise with an antirotation of the torso (see Problems With Rotation on p. 43). Use your obliques to hold your torso still despite the constant motion in the arms. Holding your torso still will reduce the range of motion in the arms.

D Work only with rotation, keeping the arms immobile and moving your body only within the machine. This variation targets the muscles responsible for rotation and core strength as well as the lower-back muscles.

E If you do not have a machine, you can do this exercise with two resistance bands set at midlevel: one in front of you and one behind you. Once you have finished the first phase, turn 180 degrees and repeat to do the other half set.

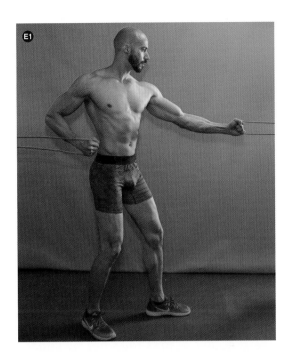

Supersets

By combining the combo twist and the jammer press without resting (see pp. 150-153), you can strengthen all of your locomotion muscles as well as your core in a very functional way in just a few minutes, all while working on your endurance as well.

Advantages

This exercise works all of the muscles in the torso without compromising the integrity of the shoulders. Doing it completely means you will have worked the muscles that pull the shoulder forward and those that pull it backward. This reduces the risk of a strength imbalance, which is often the source of injuries.

Disadvantages

Even though these machines are becoming more common in gyms, not every gym has them.

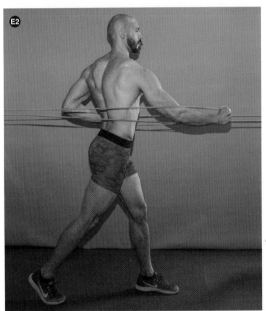

⚠ Risks

If you have low back problems, you should avoid this exercise.

Why Should an Athlete Do This Exercise?

This exercise targets the upper and middle parts of the trapezius muscles. These are strategic zones for preventing injury since they are typically difficult to strengthen.

Adjust the pulleys to about knee height. Stand facing the machine, and grab the handles using a semipronated or neutral grip ❶. Bend your arms a little to lift the shoulders as you bring the shoulder blades together by squeezing the trapezius muscles ❷. Hold the contracted position for one second before lowering the weight.

For Which Sports?

This is for all combat and contact sports, as well as those that can easily cause shoulder or neck pain, such as automobile, motorcycle, or cycling sports.

Points to Consider

As you move closer to or farther from the machine, you can change the angle at which the trapezius muscles work. To be very stable, do not keep your feet parallel; instead place one foot in front and the other behind.

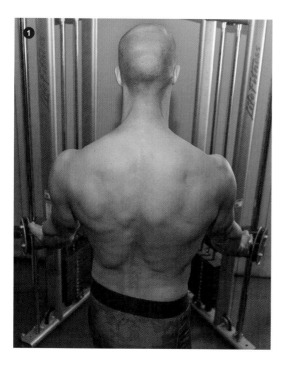
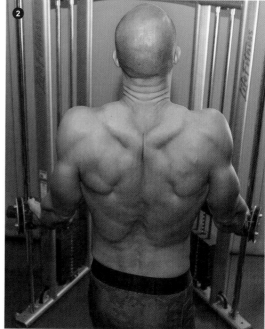

Variations

You can attach two bands in front of you at knee height **V1** for resistance **V2**, especially as a warm-up before your workout.

Advantages

The area of the trapezius muscles that is targeted here is different from the area worked during classic shrugs and from that targeted by Delavier's shrugs (for more explanation about these two exercises, see *The Strength Training Anatomy Workout,* volumes 1 through 3). This version is specifically for preventing cervical injuries.

Disadvantages

Mastering this exercise, which is more complex than it seems, requires a certain amount of learning to focus the work on the correct muscle zones.

⚠ Risks

Any strength work involving the upper-trapezius muscles is potentially dangerous for the cervical spine. Keep your head straight and slightly back. Do not let yourself become distracted, which could make you turn your head during the exercise.

Why Should an Athlete Do This Exercise?

This exercise works the abdominal muscles and the hip flexors.

For Which Sports?

This exercise is for all sports that require a powerful abdomen or in which you need to lift the leg or the knee to run faster.

Lie on your back with your legs bent and your feet tucked under a machine or a wall bar or held by a partner. Slowly lift your shoulders and peel your torso off the ground. Keep going until your torso touches your thighs. Return to the starting position and begin again, always without any jerky movements.

Variations

Ⓐ You can hold a dumbbell on your chest to increase the resistance that your muscles must overcome.

Ⓑ Instead of doing this exercise on the ground, do it on a bench. There are all kinds of benches that allow you to change the incline of your torso to make the exercise harder.

Ⓒ Instead of coming up very straight, bring your right elbow to the opposite knee and then the left elbow to the right knee. These twisting sit-ups increase the work of the obliques and augment the power of the rotator muscles as well as that of the abdominal muscles.

Ⓓ If your feet are not blocked, you can isolate the abdominal work more, but you will not be strengthening the muscles that allow you to lift your legs powerfully in the air (rectus femoris, tensor fasciae latae). This is an important loss of efficiency for many athletes.

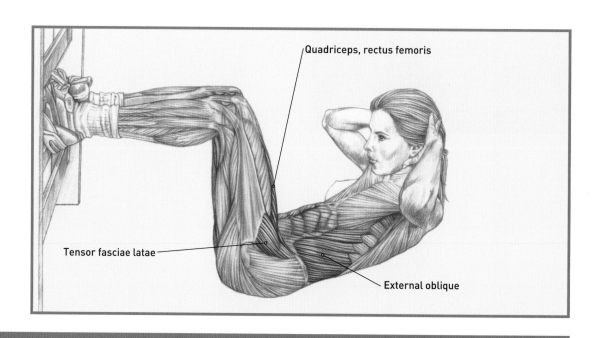

Quadriceps, rectus femoris

Tensor fasciae latae

External oblique

Advantages

Sit-ups are a more complete exercise than you might think. They allow for effective work on the hip flexors as well as the core.

Disadvantages

The rectus femoris is worked only isometrically. Sit-ups should not be the only exercise you do to get more powerful at lifting your legs.

⚠ Risks

The more you pull on your feet to target the hip flexors, the more stress you place on the low back. If you have even the slightest disc pain, it is better to avoid this exercise.

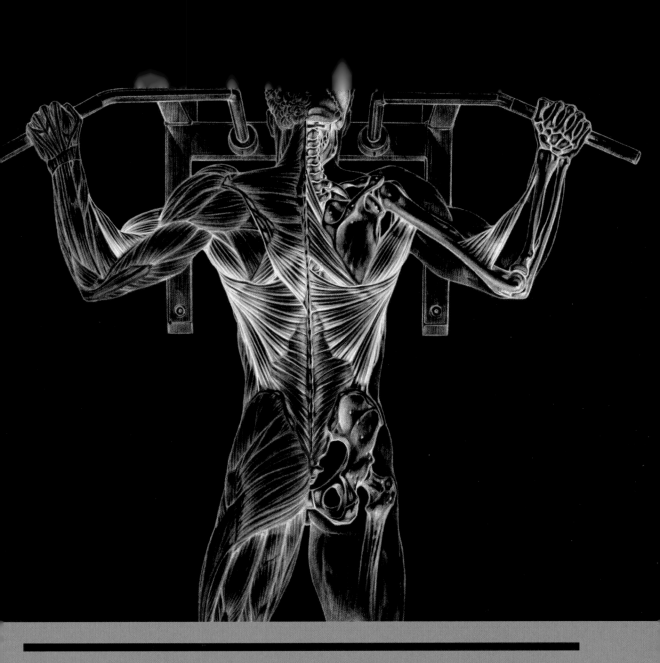

TRAINING PROGRAMS FOR PARTICULAR SPORTS

PREPARING TO WORK OUT

In this section of the book, you will find training programs for major sports for athletes of different levels. The programs are laid out in three steps:

➊ If you are just beginning strength training, use the beginner program for your sport.
➋ Once you feel comfortable with the program, move on to the advanced program.
➌ The ultimate goal is to personalize your program for maximum effectiveness by combining your experience, needs, and goals with the advice laid out in this book.

In addition to specific programs for each sport, we also provide programs to bring certain muscles up to par. For example, if you often have back pain because of your sport, then you need to focus on strengthening the muscles that support the lumbar region. Finally, we have also provided typical warm-up programs as well as recovery programs.

DO YOU NEED TO PLAN OUT YOUR WORKOUTS IN ADVANCE?

Your workouts should follow this simple logic: As you increase the training intensity for your sport, you should reduce the volume of strength training.

Similarly, after a strength training workout with heavy weights, you should have a lighter session with more reps, because a really good workout demands a longer recovery. However, a rather ineffective session is more likely to be followed by a very beneficial workout since the body will not need to dig into its reserves and will need less rest. Do not wait until you are experiencing generalized fatigue to reduce your volume of training or your weight, since by then it is too late! By adjusting your rest periods intelligently, you can avoid overtraining.

HOW MANY STRENGTH TRAINING WORKOUTS SHOULD YOU DO EACH WEEK?

A study analyzed the effects of strength training in sedentary people by comparing the effects of two, three, or four weekly training sessions over 12 weeks. Each workout included three sets of eight different exercises for the whole body.[1]

Thigh strength increased by
❂ 18 percent with two workouts,
❂ 24 percent with three workouts, and
❂ 30 percent with four workouts.

Chest strength increased by
❂ 21 percent with two workouts,
❂ 30 percent with three workouts, and
❂ 32 percent with four workouts.

With just a few sessions, you can tell that you are gaining real strength. Though more strength training sessions can give you slightly better results, performance can plateau rapidly despite a substantial increase in the volume of work. You can see that even a single strength training workout will help you make fast progress. Ideally, two trainings per week seems optimal for most beginner, or even intermediate, athletes. At the beginning, this progress occurs without putting on muscle and therefore without putting on weight. It results mostly from nervous system gains rather than from muscle hypertrophy.[1] It is possible to compensate for poor training frequency by forcing yourself to go harder in each set. But the closer you get to fatigue in an exercise, the more time you will need to recover between two workouts. If you definitely want to work out more, you can force things a little less in each set, and this will reduce the recovery time needed between workouts.[2]

WARM-UP PROGRAMS TO DO BEFORE STRENGTH TRAINING OR BEFORE PLAYING YOUR SPORT

You should do these programs before your athletic warm-up (in the field) or before a more targeted warm-up using your first strength training exercise in the gym. They will prepare not only your muscles, but also your cardiovascular system.

A WARM-UP FOR MUSCLE POTENTIATION

Using strength training exercises as a warm-up before participating in your sport has the advantage of potentiating the strength of your muscles.[3] This means that a warm-up more specific and more intense than the typical warm-up using only body weight exercises has two effects: It not only prepares your muscles but will especially boost the power of your nerve signals, making you temporarily super powerful.[4] Scientists call this state *potentiation*.

WARM-UP PROGRAM FOR THE UPPER BODY

Do one or two circuits, without resting, combining the following exercises:

1 Internal shoulder rotation with a resistance band: 20 to 50 reps
2 External shoulder rotation with a resistance band: 20 to 50 reps
3 Lateral raise: 20 to 30 reps

4 Bent-over lateral raise:
20 to 30 reps
5 Row: 20 to 30 reps

WARM-UP PROGRAM FOR SPORTS INVOLVING ROTATION

Do 1 or 2 circuits, without resting:
1 Internal shoulder rotation with a resistance band: 20 to 50 reps
2 External shoulder rotation with a resistance band: 20 to 50 reps
3 Plank:
at least 30 seconds
4 Standing ab twist
with a resistance band:
20 to 30 reps on each side
5 Bridge (hip thrust): 20 to 30 reps

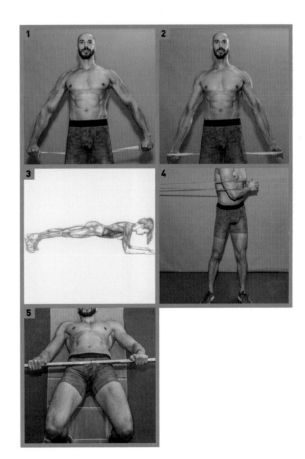

WARM-UP PROGRAM FOR THE LOWER BODY

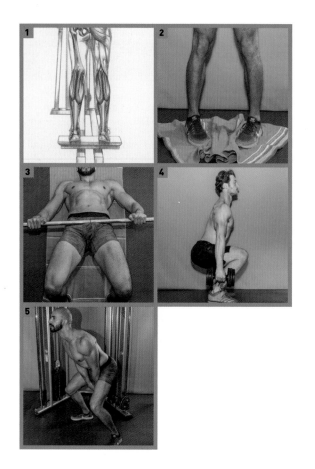

Do 1 or 2 circuits, without resting.

1 Standing calf raise:
30 to 50 reps

2 Warm-up for the hip rotators using a towel: 50 to 100 reps

3 Bridge (hip thrust):
20 to 30 reps

4 Squat with two dumbbells:
20 to 30 reps

5 Pull through: 20 to 30 reps

Do 1 or 2 circuits, without resting.

1 Internal shoulder rotation with a resistance band: 20 to 50 reps

2 External shoulder rotation with a resistance band: 20 to 50 reps

3 Standing calf raise: 30 to 50 reps

4 Row: 20 to 30 reps

5 Warm-up for the hip rotators using a towel: 50 to 100 reps

6 Bridge (hip thrust): 20 to 30 reps

7 Squat with two dumbbells: 20 to 30 reps

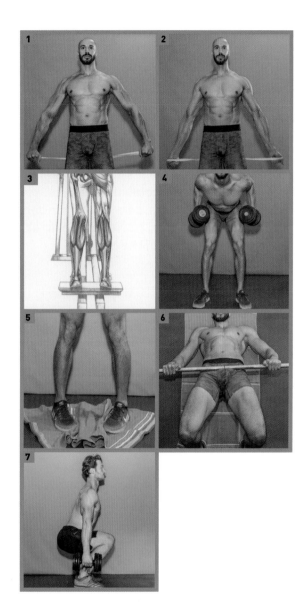

PROGRAMS TO BRING A SPECIFIC WEAK AREA UP TO PAR

If you do not wish to embark on a complete strength training program, there is a strong chance that you want to strengthen a particular area instead. This area might feel weak to you or might be causing you pain too often. The goal of these targeted programs is to work specifically on a factor that is limiting your performance. These programs can also be added to your current strength training regimen to quickly catch up a weak area.

Since the sets are combined rapidly, you will keep the weight the same from set to set, unless you feel that you can go heavier because you are doing more than the recommended number of repetitions. However, if you are below the recommended number, feel free to take some weight off of the bar.

STRENGTHEN THE SHOULDERS

Do 2 to 4 sets of the same exercise with 30 seconds to 1 minute of rest after each set. Once you complete all the sets of the first exercise, move on to the next exercise.

1 Jammer press: 10 to 12 reps
2 Bent-over lateral raise:
10 to 15 reps
3 Lateral raise: 12 to 15 reps

STRENGTHEN THE SHOULDER ROTATORS AND STABILIZERS

Do 2 to 5 circuits, without resting.
1 External shoulder rotation with a resistance band: 20 to 30 reps
2 Internal shoulder rotation with a resistance band: 20 to 30 reps
3 Bent-over lateral raise: 10 to 15 reps

INCREASE THE POWER OF TORSO ROTATION

Do 2 to 5 circuits, with a few dozen seconds of rest after each set.

1 Side plank:
at least 30 seconds
on each side
2 Twisting sit-up:
15 to 20 reps on each side
3 Standing ab twist with a resistance band:
20 to 30 reps on each side

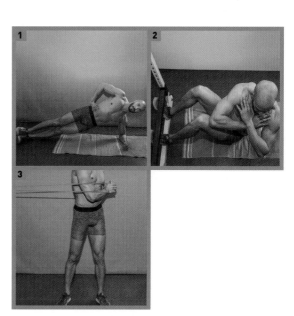

STRENGTHEN THE CORE

Do 3 circuits, with the minimum amount of rest possible.

1 Sit-up: 20 to 30 reps
2 Side plank:
at least 30 seconds
on each side
3 Twisting sit-up:
20 to 30 reps on each side
4 Plank: at least 1 minute

STRENGTHEN THE ADDUCTORS

Do 2 to 5 circuits, with a few dozen seconds of rest after each set.

1 Hip adduction:
20 to 30 reps
2 Side lunge:
12 to 20 reps per leg
3 Bent-knee leg lift with hip rotation to work the sartorius: 30 to 50 reps per leg

STRENGTHEN THE UPPER BACK

Do 2 to 4 sets of the same exercise with 30 seconds to 1 minute of rest after each set. Once you complete all the sets of the first exercise, move on to the next exercise.

1 Pull-up: 8 to 12 reps
2 Bent-over lateral raise:
10 to 15 reps
3 Shrug using an adjustable pulley:
20 to 30 reps

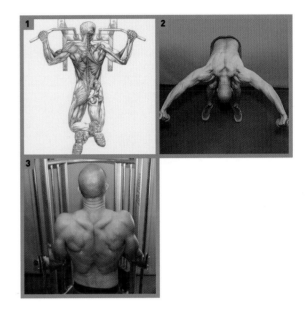

STRENGTHEN THE LOWER BACK

Do 2 to 4 sets of the same exercise with 30 seconds to 1 minute of rest after each set. Once you complete all the sets of the first exercise, move on to the next exercise.

1 Row: 12 to 20 reps
2 GHR: 10 to 15 reps
3 Bridge (hip thrust): 20 to 30 reps

WEAKNESS IN THE LUMBAR MUSCLES AND ELEVATED BODY WEIGHT: TWO CUMULATIVE FACTORS IN THE RISK OF INJURY

The combination of weak lumbar muscles and elevated body weight promotes back pain. This combination is also associated with a greater incidence of leg injuries.[5] It is essential to strengthen the lower back, even more so if you are heavy and your opponents are trying to make you fall, as in rugby or American football, for example.

GET STRONGER AT PULLING WITH YOUR ARMS

For the first two exercises, do 2 to 4 sets with 30 seconds to 1 minute of rest after each set. Once you have completed all the sets for the first exercise, move on to the next exercise. Combine the last two exercises three or four times in a circuit, with no rest breaks.

1 Pull-up: 6 to 12 reps
2 Row: 10 to 15 reps
3 Reverse curl: 15 to 20 reps
4 Wrist curl: 20 to 30 reps

DO YOU NEED TO TRAIN YOUR LEFT ARM IF YOU USE ONLY YOUR RIGHT ARM?

Our answer is obviously yes. Studies have shown that the body reacts bilaterally to all physical demands. For example, when you pull with the muscles on your right side, the muscles on your left side will also become more flexible, although to a lesser degree. Doing strength training on the right side will also increase strength in the muscles of the left side. These bilateral benefits from unilateral training can be explained by the adaptation of the central nervous system, which is trying to balance the right and left sides of the body. Therefore, we recommend training both arms, both legs, and so on equally to help the body maintain balance on both sides.

One of the benefits of this bilateralism is that in the case of serious injury or pain that prevents you from working your right side, let's say, your right side will still benefit from your training your left side. For instance, strength training for a single arm for three weeks increased the strength of that arm by 29 percent. Astonishingly, the strength of the arm that did nothing still increased by 18 percent. This nervous system adaptation delays the loss of strength of an immobilized limb.[6]

GET STRONGER AT PUSHING WITH YOUR ARMS

Do 2 to 4 sets of the same exercise with 30 seconds to 1 minute of rest after each set. Once you have completed all the sets for the first exercise, move on to the next exercise.

1 Jammer press: 10 to 12 reps
2 JM press: 10 to 15 reps
3 Wrist extension: 20 to 30 reps

STRENGTHEN THE INSIDE
OF THE FOREARM TO PREVENT GOLF ELBOW

Do 4 circuits, with a minimum amount of rest.
1 Finger flexion using a hand grip strengthener: 50 to 100 reps
2 Wrist curl: 20 to 30 reps

STRENGTHEN THE OUTSIDE OF THE FOREARM TO PREVENT TENNIS ELBOW

Do 3 circuits, with a minimum amount of rest.

1 Fingezr extension:
50 to 100 reps

2 Wrist extension: 20 to 30 reps

3 Reverse curl: 15 to 20 reps

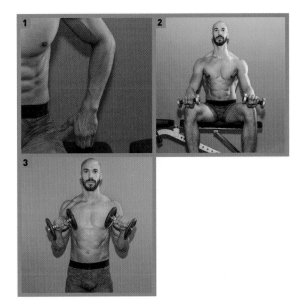

PROTECT YOUR NECK

Do 4 circuits, with a minimum amount of rest.

1 Shrug using an adjustable pulley:
20 to 30 reps

2 Lateral raise, arms as high as possible:
15 to 20 reps

STRENGTHEN THE HIP ROTATOR MUSCLES

Do 2 to 5 circuits, with a minimum amount of rest.
1 Warm-up for the hip rotators using a towel: 30 to 50 reps
2 Internal hip rotation: 20 to 30 reps
3 External hip rotation: 20 to 30 reps

SPECIAL NOTE

This specific program is essential for male athletes, but it is even more important for female athletes, since in women, the strength of the hip rotator muscles plays an important role in protecting the cruciate ligaments.[7] In female basketball players, regularly training the hip rotator muscles greatly reduces the risk of cruciate ligament injuries.[8] This strength is also very useful in combatting ankle injuries, because strengthening the hip rotator muscles is associated with better ankle stability.[9]

PROTECT THE KNEES

Do 3 circuits, with a minimum amount of rest.

1 Leg curl, lying down or seated: 10 to 15 reps

2 Warm-up for the hip rotators using a towel: 30 to 50 reps

3 Standing calf raise: 20 to 30 reps

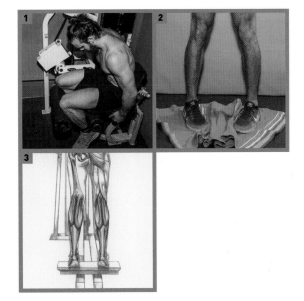

SPECIAL NOTE

This is a program only to prevent injuries! It can in no way replace reeducation following a tear in one of the cruciate ligaments of the knees. In that case, only surgery can repair the damage. This is why it is so important to prevent these kinds of injuries, which are unfortunately very common in certain sports.

Do 3 circuits, with a minimum amount of rest.

1 Razor curl (do only the descent): 15 to 20 reps

2 Pull through: 12 to 20 reps

3 Leg press, feet high on the platform: 8 to 12 reps

4 Leg curl, lying down or seated: 10 to 15 reps

HAMSTRING TEARS

In all sports that require running, hamstring tears are both frequent and debilitating. For professional soccer players, two huge risk factors for injuries are a lack of eccentric strength in the hamstrings and a strength imbalance between strong quadriceps muscles and weak hamstrings.[10] If these kinds of imbalances can be found in professional athletes, then they are probably even more common among amateur athletes. A good strength training program should be able to balance things out.

MAKE YOUR THIGHS MORE POWERFUL

Do 2 to 4 sets of the same exercise with 30 seconds to 1 minute of rest after each set. Once you have completed all the sets for the first exercise, move on to the next exercise.

1 Squat with a trap bar or with dumbbells: 6 to 8 reps

2 Leg curl, lying down or seated: 10 to 15 reps

3 Bridge (hip thrust): 20 to 30 reps

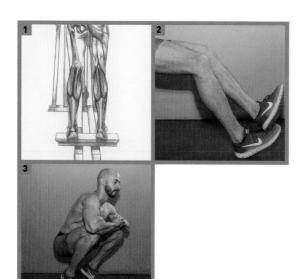

Do 3 circuits, with a minimum amount of rest.

1 Standing calf raise:
20 to 30 reps

2 Toe raise:
20 negative reps

3 Crouching calf raise:
30 to 50 reps

ACHILLES' TENDON RUPTURE

With the exception of ruptures caused by degeneration of the tendon due to age, Achilles' tendon ruptures are largely caused by sporting activities, especially ball sports.[11] These ruptures happen when athletes must suddenly sprint or jump. You must increase the tendon's resistance to tearing during stretching, so you need to focus on eccentric strength in the tendon rather than flexibility.

STRENGTHEN THE BONES TO AVOID FRACTURES IN SPORTS WHERE YOU COULD FALL OR IN CONTACT SPORTS

Do 2 or 3 sets of the same exercise with 30 seconds to 1 minute of rest after each set. Once all the sets of the first exercise are complete, move on to the next exercise.

1 Lateral raise:
15 to 20 reps
2 Squat with two dumbbells:
10 to 15 reps
3 Bench press: 10 to 15 reps
4 Reverse curl: 15 to 20 reps
5 Standing calf raise:
15 to 20 reps
6 GHR: 15 to 20 reps

TRAINING PROGRAMS FOR RUNNING SPORTS

TRAINING FOR A SPRINTER WHO IS TENDINOUS

■ PRIMARY MUSCLE GROUPS WORKED

Sprints provide intense work for the lower body, the core muscles, and the muscles that rotate the torso. The more tendinous an athlete is, the more that athlete uses the glutes and hamstrings. This athlete does not suffer from too much calf work.

■ ZONES TO STRENGTHEN TO PREVENT INJURIES

The most frequent injuries affect the entire back, the hip rotator muscles, the knees, the hamstrings, and the ankles.

■ NECESSARY MUSCLE QUALITIES

Sprints require explosiveness. It is a good idea to train in normal sets, using the number of repetitions appropriate for the distance you run:

- ✪ 4 to 6 reps for the 60 meter
- ✪ 6 to 10 reps for the 100 meter
- ✪ 20 to 30 reps for the 400 meter

Rest for a few minutes between exercises, but reduce the rest time by a few seconds if you are training for the 400 meter since that distance requires more endurance than the 100 meter.

BEGINNER PROGRAM

Train 1 or 2 times weekly.
1 Lunge: 4 sets per leg
2 Twisting sit-up: 4 sets per side
3 GHR: 3 sets

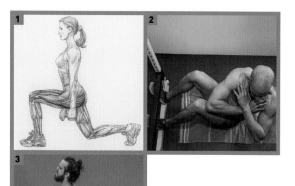

4 Leg curl, lying down: 3 sets
5 Standing calf raise: 4 sets

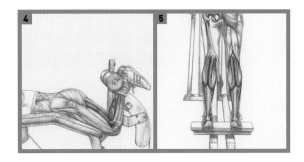

ADVANCED PROGRAM

Train at least twice weekly.
1 Lunge: 5 sets per leg
2 Bent-knee leg lift, standing, trying
to go as high as possible:
4 sets per leg
3 Bridge (hip thrust): 4 sets
4 Twisting sit-up: 4 sets per side
5 GHR: 3 sets
6 Standing calf raise: 5 sets
7 Leg curl, lying down: 3 sets

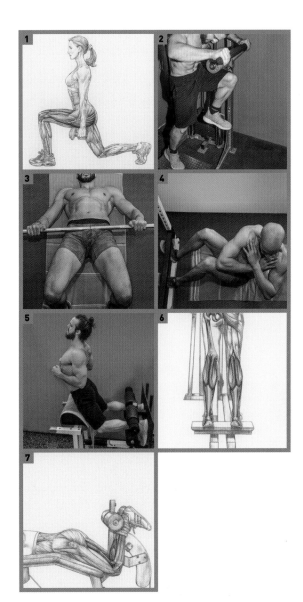

TRAINING FOR A SPRINTER WHO IS MUSCULAR

■ PRIMARY MUSCLE GROUPS WORKED

Sprints provide intense work for the lower body, the core muscles, and the muscles that rotate the torso. The more muscular an athlete is, the more that athlete will use the quadriceps and will experience intense calf work; therefore, these athletes should focus on the hip flexors.

■ ZONES TO STRENGTHEN TO PREVENT INJURIES

The most frequent injuries affect the entire back, the hip rotator muscles, the knees, the hamstrings, and the ankles.

■ NECESSARY MUSCLE QUALITIES

Sprints require explosiveness. It is a good idea to train in normal sets, using the number of repetitions appropriate for the distance you run:

✪ 6 to 8 reps for the 60 meter
✪ 8 to 12 reps for the 100 meter
✪ 20 to 30 reps for the 400 meter

Rest for a few minutes between exercises, but reduce the rest time by a few seconds if you are training for the 400 meter since that distance requires more endurance than the 100 meter.

BEGINNER PROGRAM

Train 1 or 2 times weekly.
1 Lunge: 4 sets per leg
2 Bent-knee leg lift, standing, trying to go as high as possible:
4 sets per leg
3 GHR: 3 sets

4 Twisting sit-up:
4 sets on each side
5 Leg curl, lying down: 3 sets

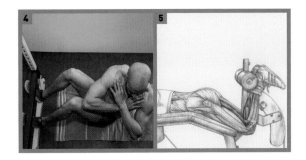

ADVANCED PROGRAM

Train at least twice weekly.
1 Lunge: 5 sets per leg
2 Bent-knee leg lift, standing, trying
to go as high as possible:
5 sets per leg
3 GHR: 3 sets
4 Twisting sit-up: 4 sets on each side
5 Leg press: 3 sets
6 Leg curl, lying down: 3 sets

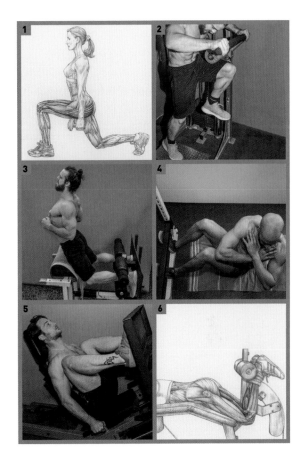

■ PRIMARY MUSCLE GROUPS WORKED

Hurdles provide intense work for the lower body, the core, and the hip rotator muscles. The higher the hurdle, the more important the hip flexors and the abductors are. It is also beneficial to have very flexible hips.

■ ZONES TO STRENGTHEN TO PREVENT INJURIES

The most frequent injuries affect the entire back, the shoulders, the hip rotator muscles, the knees, the hamstrings, and the ankles.

■ NECESSARY MUSCLE QUALITIES

Hurdles require flexibility and explosiveness. It is a good idea to train in normal sets, using the number of repetitions appropriate for the distance you run:

- ✪ 6 to 8 reps for the 60 meter
- ✪ 10 to 15 reps for the 110 meter
- ✪ 20 to 30 reps for the 400 meter

Rest for a few minutes between exercises, but reduce the rest time by a few seconds if you are training for the 400 meter since that distance requires more endurance than the 110 meter.

BEGINNER PROGRAM

Train 1 or 2 times weekly.
1 Side lunge: 4 sets per leg
2 Bent-knee leg lift, standing, trying to go as high as possible:
4 sets per leg
3 GHR: 3 sets
4 Twisting sit-up: 4 sets on each side

ADVANCED PROGRAM

Train at least twice weekly.
1 Side lunge: 5 sets per leg
2 Bent-knee leg lift, standing, trying
to go as high as possible:
5 sets per leg
3 GHR: 4 sets
4 Hip abduction: 5 sets
5 Twisting sit-up: 5 sets on each side
6 Standing calf raise: 5 sets

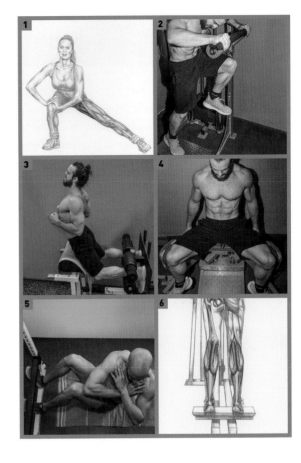

■ PRIMARY MUSCLE GROUPS WORKED

The high jump provides intense work for the lower body, the core, and the hip and torso rotator muscles.

■ ZONES TO STRENGTHEN TO PREVENT INJURIES

The most frequent injuries affect the entire back, the abdominal muscles, the hip rotator muscles, the knees, and the ankles.

■ NECESSARY MUSCLE QUALITIES

The high jump requires flexibility and explosiveness. It is a good idea to train in very short, normal sets of 4 to 12 reps. Rest for a few minutes between sets and between different exercises.

BEGINNER PROGRAM

Train 1 or 2 times weekly.
1 Lunge: 4 sets of 6 to 10 reps per leg
2 Bent-knee leg lift, standing, trying to go as high as possible:
3 sets of 4 to 8 reps per leg
3 GHR: 4 sets of 10 to 12 reps
4 Twisting sit-up: 3 sets of 10 to 12 reps per side

ADVANCED PROGRAM

Train at least twice weekly.
1 Lunge: 4 sets of 6 to 10 reps
per leg
2 Bent-knee leg lift, standing, trying
to go as high as possible:
3 sets of 4 to 6 reps per leg
3 GHR: 4 sets of 10 to 12 reps
4 Standing calf raise: 4 sets of
8 to 12 reps
5 Twisting sit-up: 3 sets of 10 to 12 reps
per side
6 Bridge (hip thrust): 4 sets of 6 to 10 reps

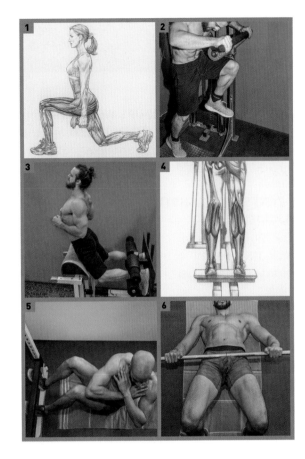

LONG JUMP AND TRIPLE JUMP

■ PRIMARY MUSCLE GROUPS WORKED

These jumps provide intense work for the lower body, the core, the shoulder, and the hip and torso rotator muscles.

■ ZONES TO STRENGTHEN TO PREVENT INJURIES

The most frequent injuries affect the lower back, the abdominal muscles, the hip rotator muscles, the hamstrings, the knees, and the ankles.

■ NECESSARY MUSCLE QUALITIES

These jumps require flexibility and explosiveness. It is a good idea to train in very short, normal sets of 4 to 12 reps. Rest for a few minutes between sets and between different exercises.

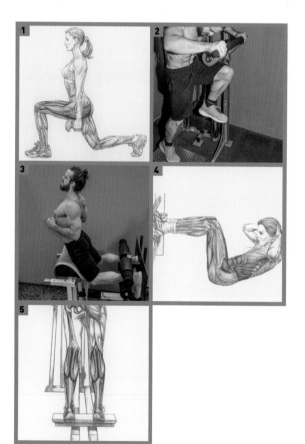

BEGINNER PROGRAM

Train 1 or 2 times weekly.
1 Lunge: 4 sets of 8 to 12 reps per leg
2 Bent-knee leg lift, standing, trying to go as high as possible:
3 sets of 4 to 8 reps per leg
3 GHR: 4 sets of 10 to 12 reps
4 Sit-up: 4 sets of 10 to 12 reps
5 Standing calf raise: 4 sets of 8 to 12 reps

ADVANCED PROGRAM

Train at least twice weekly.

1 Lunge: 4 sets of 8 to 12 reps
per leg

2 Bent-knee leg lift, standing, trying
to go as high as possible:
3 sets of 4 to 8 reps per leg

3 GHR: 4 sets of 10 to 12 reps

4 Bench press: 4 sets of
8 to 12 reps

5 Bridge (hip thrust): 4 sets of
8 to 12 reps

6 Sit-up: 4 sets of 10 to 12 reps

7 Standing calf raise: 4 sets of 8 to 12 reps

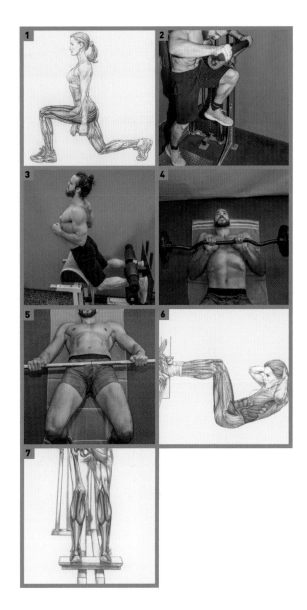

POLE VAULT

■ PRIMARY MUSCLE GROUPS WORKED

The pole vault provides intense work for the lower body, the core, and the hip and torso rotator muscles, as well as the arms via the back and shoulders.

■ ZONES TO STRENGTHEN TO PREVENT INJURIES

The most frequent injuries affect the whole back, the elbows, the wrists, the shoulders, the abdominal muscles, the hip rotator muscles, the knees, and the ankles.

■ NECESSARY MUSCLE QUALITIES

Pole vaulting requires flexibility and explosiveness. It is a good idea to train in very short, normal sets of 4 to 12 reps. Rest for a few minutes between sets and between different exercises.

BEGINNER PROGRAM

Train 1 or 2 times weekly.
1 Lunge: 4 sets of 8 to 12 reps per leg
2 Row: 4 sets of 8 to 12 reps
3 GHR: 4 sets of 10 to 12 reps
4 Twisting sit-up: 3 sets of 10 to 12 reps per side
5 Standing calf raise: 4 sets of 8 to 12 reps

ADVANCED PROGRAM

Train at least twice weekly.

1 Lunge: 4 sets of 8 to 12 reps
per leg

2 Row: 4 sets of 8 to 12 reps

3 Bent-knee leg lift, standing, trying
to go as high as possible:
3 sets of 10 to 12 reps per leg

4 GHR: 4 sets of 10 to 12 reps

5 JM press: 4 sets of 8 to 12 reps

6 Twisting sit-up: 3 sets of 10 to 12 reps
per side

7 Standing calf raise: 4 sets of 8 to 12 reps

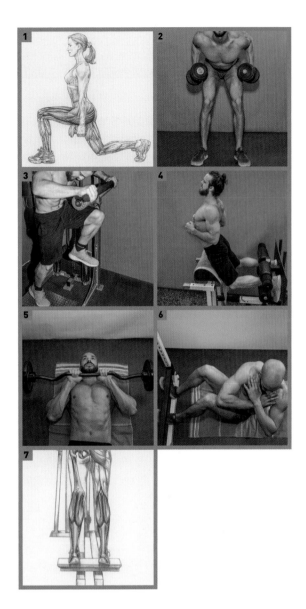

■ PRIMARY MUSCLE GROUPS WORKED

Running provides intense work for the lower body, the core, and the torso rotator muscles.

■ ZONES TO STRENGTHEN TO PREVENT INJURIES

The most frequent injuries affect the lower back, the hip rotator muscles, the knees, the hamstrings, and the ankles.

■ NECESSARY MUSCLE QUALITIES

Running requires explosiveness and endurance. It is best to train in circuits, using the number of repetitions appropriate for the distance you run:

- ✪ 20 to 30 reps for the 800 meter
- ✪ 30 to 40 reps for the 1,500 meter
- ✪ About 50 reps for longer distances

Do not rest for very long (a few dozen seconds maximum) between exercises and circuits.

BEGINNER PROGRAM

Train 1 or 2 times weekly. Do 2 or 3 circuits.

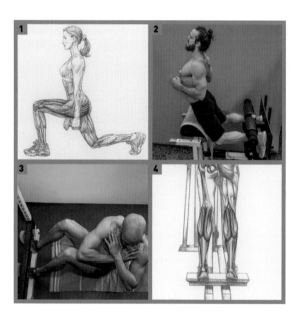

1 Lunges
2 GHR
3 Twisting sit-up
4 Standing calf raise

ADVANCED PROGRAM

Train at least twice weekly. Do 3 or 4 circuits.

1 Lunge
2 Bent-knee leg lift, standing
3 GHR
4 Twisting sit-up
5 Leg curl, lying down

■ PRIMARY MUSCLE GROUPS WORKED

Racewalking provides intense work for the lower body, the torso rotator muscles, and the core. The core's purpose is not only to support the back and pull in the stomach; in endurance athletes, studies have shown that abdominal weakness is associated with a higher rate of side stitches.[12] The stronger your transversus abdominis muscle is, the fewer side stitches you will have. Strengthening the core muscles is a good strategy to reduce the frequency of this type of pain.

■ ZONES TO STRENGTHEN TO PREVENT INJURIES

The most frequent injuries affect the lower back, the hip rotator muscles, the knees, and the ankles.

■ NECESSARY MUSCLE QUALITIES

Racewalking requires endurance. It is best to train in circuits and not rest too much between exercises and circuits.

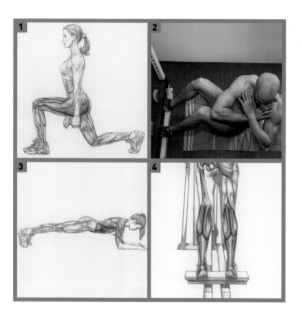

BEGINNER PROGRAM

Train 1 or 2 times weekly. Do 2 or 3 circuits.

1 Lunge: 30 to 50 reps per leg
2 Twisting sit-up: 25 to 30 reps
on each side
3 Plank:
at least 1 minute
4 Standing calf raise: 30 to 50 reps

ADVANCED PROGRAM

Train at least twice weekly. Do 3 or 4 circuits.

1 Lunge: 30 to 50 reps per leg
2 GHR: 20 to 30 reps
3 Twisting sit-up: 25 to 30 reps on each side
4 Bridge (hip thrust):
30 to 50 reps
5 Plank: at least 1 minute

TRAINING PROGRAMS FOR TEAM BALL SPORTS

SOCCER

■ PRIMARY MUSCLE GROUPS WORKED
Soccer provides intense work for the lower body as well as the torso and hip rotator muscles.

■ ZONES TO STRENGTHEN TO PREVENT INJURIES
The most frequent injuries affect the lower back, the hip rotator muscles, the hamstrings, the knees, and the ankles.

■ NECESSARY MUSCLE QUALITIES
An analysis of high-level soccer matches over the past 10 years shows that the quantity of sprints has increased from 30 percent to 80 percent. This requires players to increase their speed and explosiveness and underscores the growing importance of strength training.[13]

Soccer requires not only explosiveness, but also endurance. It is best to train in circuits using average-length sets and to rest for a few dozen seconds between exercises and circuits.

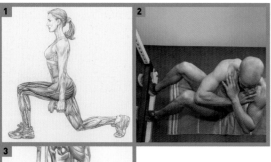

BEGINNER PROGRAM

Train 1 or 2 times weekly. Do 3 to 6 circuits.

1 Lunge: 12 to 20 reps per leg
2 Twisting sit-up: 12 to 20 reps on each side
3 Standing calf raise: 20 to 30 reps

4 Hip adduction:
20 to 30 reps
5 Hip abduction:
20 to 30 reps

ADVANCED PROGRAM

Train at least twice weekly. Do 3 or 4 circuits.

1 Lunge: 12 to 20 reps per leg
2 Twisting sit-up: 12 to 20 reps on each side
3 Standing calf raise:
20 to 30 reps
4 Hip adduction:
20 to 30 reps
5 Bent-knee leg lift with hip rotation to work the sartorius: 20 to 30 reps per leg
6 Hip abduction:
20 to 30 reps
7 GHR: 20 to 30 reps

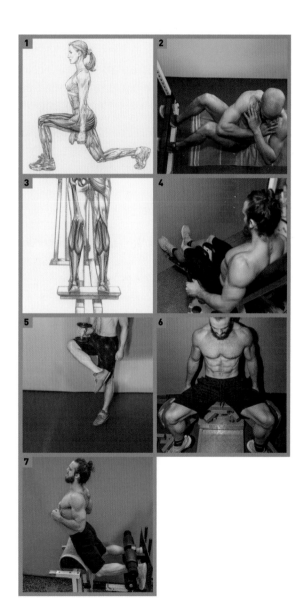

RUGBY

■ **PRIMARY MUSCLE GROUPS WORKED**
Rugby works the entire body intensely, but especially the legs and the torso and hip rotator muscles.

■ **ZONES TO STRENGTHEN TO PREVENT INJURIES**
The most frequent injuries affect the entire back, the shoulders, the hip rotator muscles, the hamstrings, the knees, and the ankles.

■ **NECESSARY MUSCLE QUALITIES**
Rugby requires not only explosiveness, but also strength and endurance. It is best to train in circuits using an average number of reps and to rest for a few dozen seconds between exercises and circuits.

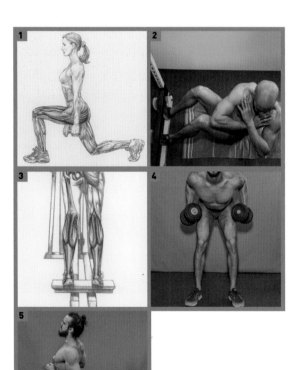

BEGINNER PROGRAM

Train 1 or 2 times weekly. Do 3 to 6 circuits.

1 Lunge: 12 to 20 reps per leg
2 Twisting sit-up: 12 to 20 reps on each side
3 Standing calf raise: 12 to 20 reps
4 Row: 12 to 20 reps
5 GHR: 20 to 30 reps

ADVANCED PROGRAM

Train at least twice weekly. Do 3 or 4 circuits.

1 Lunge: 12 to 20 reps per leg
2 Twisting sit-up: 12 to 20 reps on each side
3 Leg curl, lying down or seated: 10 to 15 reps
4 Row: 12 to 20 reps
5 GHR: 20 to 30 reps
6 Shrug using an adjustable pulley: 12 to 20 reps
7 Standing calf raise: 12 to 20 reps

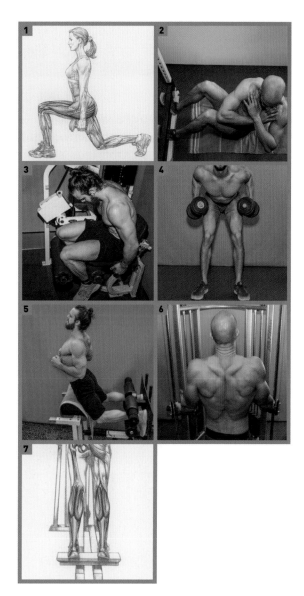

AMERICAN FOOTBALL

■ PRIMARY MUSCLE GROUPS WORKED

American football provides intense work for the entire body, especially the legs and the torso and hip rotator muscles, as well as the arms via the chest, triceps, and shoulders.

■ ZONES TO STRENGTHEN TO PREVENT INJURIES

The most frequent injuries affect the entire back, the shoulders, the hip rotator muscles, the hamstrings, the knees, and the ankles.

■ NECESSARY MUSCLE QUALITIES

American football requires not only explosiveness, but also strength and endurance. It is best to train in circuits using an average number of reps and to rest for a few dozen seconds between exercises. Take a couple of minutes to rest after each circuit instead of starting the next circuit right away.

BEGINNER PROGRAM

Train 1 or 2 times weekly. Do 3 to 6 circuits.

1 Lunge: 12 to 20 reps per leg
2 Twisting sit-up: 12 to 20 reps on each side
3 Squat with a trap bar or with dumbbells: 8 to 12 reps
4 Jammer press: 10 to 12 reps
5 GHR: 20 to 30 reps

ADVANCED PROGRAM

Train at least twice weekly. Do 3 or 4 circuits.

1 Lunge: 12 to 20 reps per leg
2 Twisting sit-up: 12 to 20 reps on each side
3 Squat with a trap bar or with dumbbells: 8 to 12 reps
4 Jammer press: 6 to 10 reps
5 GHR: 20 to 30 reps
6 Shrug using an adjustable pulley: 12 to 20 reps
7 JM press: 6 to 10 reps

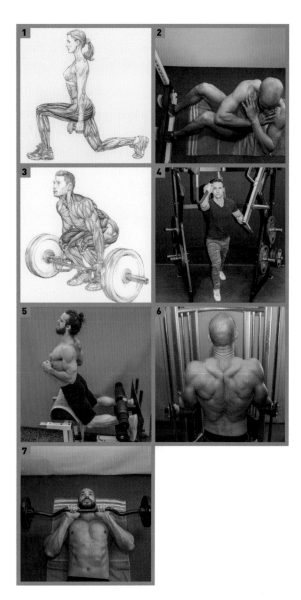

BASKETBALL

■ PRIMARY MUSCLE GROUPS WORKED

Basketball provides intense work for the lower body; the arms via the shoulders, the chest, and the back; and the torso and hip rotator muscles.

■ ZONES TO STRENGTHEN TO PREVENT INJURIES

The most frequent injuries affect the shoulders, the back, the hip rotator muscles, the hamstrings, the knees, and the ankles.

■ NECESSARY MUSCLE QUALITIES

Basketball requires explosiveness and endurance. It is best to train in circuits using an average number of reps and to rest for a few dozen seconds between exercises and circuits.

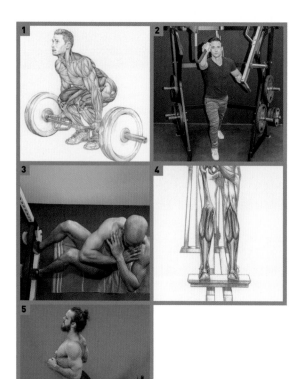

BEGINNER PROGRAM

Train 1 or 2 times weekly. Do 3 to 6 circuits.

1 Squat with a trap bar or with dumbbells: 8 to 12 reps
2 Jammer press: 10 to 12 reps
3 Twisting sit-up: 12 to 20 reps on each side
4 Standing calf raise: 20 to 30 reps
5 GHR: 20 to 30 reps

ADVANCED PROGRAM

Train at least twice weekly. Do 3 or 4 circuits.

1 Squat with a trap bar or with dumbbells:
8 to 12 reps
2 Jammer press: 10 to 12 reps
3 Bent-over lateral raise:
10 to 15 reps
4 Twisting sit-up: 12 to 20 reps on each
side
5 Pull through: 12 to 20 reps
6 Standing calf raise:
20 to 30 reps
7 GHR: 20 to 30 reps

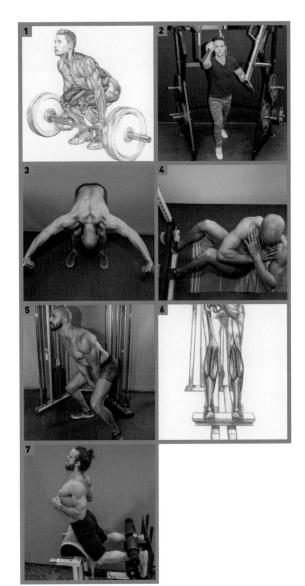

■ PRIMARY MUSCLE GROUPS WORKED

Handball provides intense work for the lower body; the arms via the shoulders, the chest, and the back; and the torso and hip rotator muscles.

■ ZONES TO STRENGTHEN TO PREVENT INJURIES

The most frequent injuries affect the shoulders, the back, the hip rotator muscles, the hamstrings, the knees, and the ankles.

■ NECESSARY MUSCLE QUALITIES

Handball requires explosiveness and endurance. It is best to train in circuits using an average number of reps and to rest for a few dozen seconds between exercises and circuits.

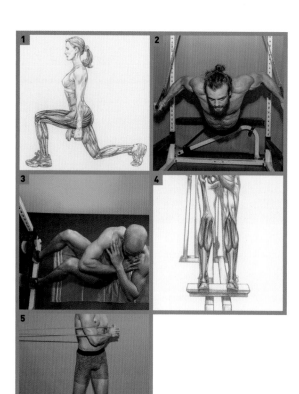

BEGINNER PROGRAM

Train 1 or 2 times weekly. Do 3 to 6 circuits.

1 Lunge: 12 to 20 reps per leg
2 Ring fly: 6 to 10 reps
3 Twisting sit-up: 12 to 20 reps on each side
4 Standing calf raise: 20 to 30 reps
5 Standing ab twist with a resistance band: 20 to 30 reps on each side

ADVANCED PROGRAM

Train at least twice weekly. Do 3 or 4 circuits.

1 Lunge: 12 to 20 reps per leg
2 Ring fly: 6 to 10 reps
3 Bent-over lateral raise:
10 to 15 reps
4 Twisting sit-up: 12 to 20 reps on each
side
5 Standing ab twist
with a resistance band:
20 to 30 reps on each side
6 Standing calf raise:
20 to 30 reps
7 GHR: 20 to 30 reps

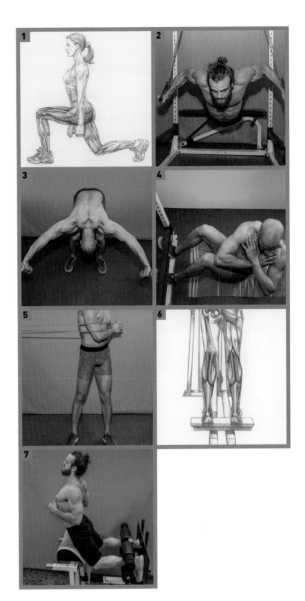

■ PRIMARY MUSCLE GROUPS WORKED

Volleyball provides intense work for the lower body; the arms via the shoulders, the chest, and the back; and the torso and hip rotator muscles.

■ ZONES TO STRENGTHEN TO PREVENT INJURIES

The most frequent injuries affect the shoulders, the back, the hip rotator muscles, the hamstrings, the knees, and the ankles. In volleyball players, including high-level players, atrophy of the infraspinatus is often found. This promotes shoulder injuries.[14] Only strength training can reduce this specific injury factor and thus prolong an athlete's career.

■ NECESSARY MUSCLE QUALITIES

Volleyball requires explosiveness and endurance. It is best to train in circuits using an average number of reps and to rest for a few dozen seconds between exercises and circuits.

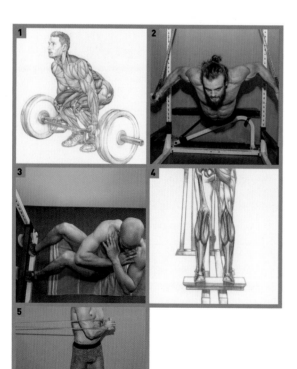

BEGINNER PROGRAM

Train 1 or 2 times weekly. Do 3 to 6 circuits.

1 Squat with a trap bar or with dumbbells: 8 to 12 reps
2 Ring fly: 6 to 10 reps
3 Twisting sit-up: 12 to 20 reps on each side
4 Standing calf raise: 20 to 30 reps
5 Standing ab twist with a resistance band: 20 to 30 reps on each side

ADVANCED PROGRAM

Train at least twice weekly. Do 3 or 4 circuits.

1 Squat with a trap bar or with dumbbells:
8 to 12 reps
2 Ring fly: 6 to 10 reps
3 Bent-over lateral raise:
10 to 15 reps
4 Twisting sit-up: 12 to 20 reps on each side
5 Jammer press: 10 to 12 reps
6 Standing calf raise:
20 to 30 reps
7 GHR: 20 to 30 reps

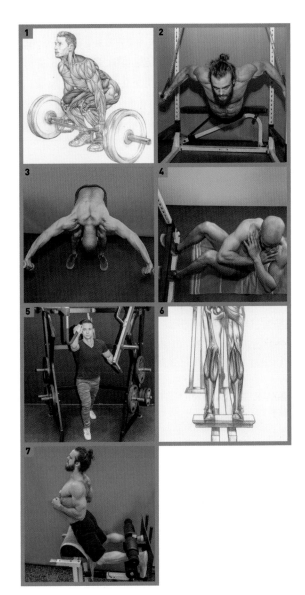

TRAINING PROGRAMS FOR GOLF AND SPORTS INVOLVING ROTATION

GOLF

■ PRIMARY MUSCLE GROUPS WORKED

Golf works the torso via the torso rotator muscles, the arms via the shoulders and back, and stability via the core muscles and legs. Stiffer muscles, especially in the thighs, increase the power of your swing.[15]

■ ZONES TO STRENGTHEN TO PREVENT INJURIES

The most frequent injuries affect the shoulders, the back, the hip rotator muscles, and the forearms.

■ NECESSARY MUSCLE QUALITIES

Golf requires explosiveness and endurance. It is best to train in circuits using an average number of reps and to rest for a few dozen seconds between exercises and circuits.

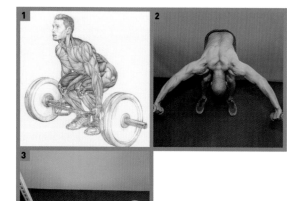

BEGINNER PROGRAM

Train 1 or 2 times weekly. Do 3 to 6 circuits.

1 Squat with a trap bar or with dumbbells: 8 to 12 reps
2 Bent-over lateral raise: 10 to 15 reps
3 Twisting sit-up: 12 to 20 reps on each side

4 External shoulder rotation:
20 to 30 reps
5 Plank: at least 1 minute

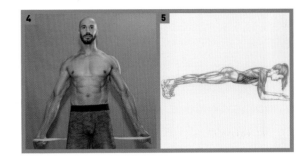

ADVANCED PROGRAM

Train at least twice weekly. Do 3 or 4 circuits.

1 Squat with a trap bar or with dumbbells:
8 to 12 reps
2 Standing ab twist
with a resistance band:
20 to 30 reps on each side
3 Bent-over lateral raise:
10 to 15 reps
4 Twisting sit-up: 12 to 20 reps on each
side
5 External shoulder rotation:
20 to 30 reps
6 Plank:
at least 1 minute
7 GHR: 20 to 30 reps

■ PRIMARY MUSCLE GROUPS WORKED

Archery works the upper body, especially the shoulders, arms, and forearms. However, both good support of the torso and rotation are required, along with good stability in the legs. Since the spine serves as a link between the arms and the legs, the abdominal muscles are heavily recruited, both for core support and for antirotation.

■ ZONES TO STRENGTHEN TO PREVENT INJURIES

The most frequent injuries affect the shoulders and the forearms.[16] It is extremely important to do a specific warm-up for the rotator cuff before any training or workout.

■ NECESSARY MUSCLE QUALITIES

This is, above all, a sport that requires explosive power, but power that lasts over time, which also involves endurance. It is best to train using short, normal sets and to take a rest period that corresponds to your shooting frequency.

BEGINNER PROGRAM

Train 1 or 2 times weekly. Do 3 to 6 circuits.

1 Bent-over lateral raise: 10 to 15 reps
2 Row: 15 to 20 reps
3 GHR: 20 to 30 reps

4 Reverse curl: 15 to 20 reps
5 Standing ab twist with a resistance band and the arms in antirotation: 20 to 30 reps on each side

ADVANCED PROGRAM

Train at least twice weekly. Do 3 or 4 circuits.

1 Front raise:
6 to 12 reps
2 Row: 15 to 20 reps
3 Wrist curl: 20 to 30 reps
4 Squat with a trap bar or with dumbbells:
8 to 12 reps
5 GHR: 20 to 30 reps
6 Finger extension:
20 to 30 reps
7 Finger flexion using a hand grip strengthener: 20 to 30 reps

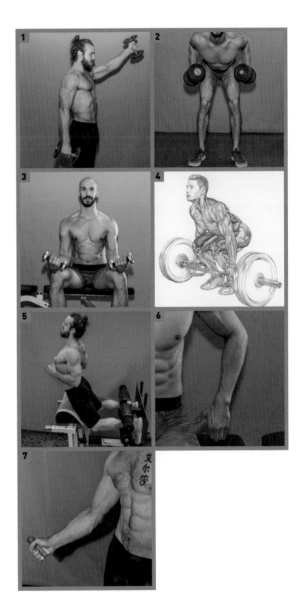

TRAINING PROGRAMS FOR SWIMMING AND NAUTICAL SPORTS

CRAWL

■ PRIMARY MUSCLE GROUPS WORKED

The crawl stroke works the upper body intensely, and the muscles in the lower body are primarily working via the hip extensor muscles. The crawl stroke also requires powerful torso rotation.

■ ZONES TO STRENGTHEN TO PREVENT INJURIES

The most frequent injuries occur in the shoulders.

■ NECESSARY MUSCLE QUALITIES

The crawl stroke requires strength and endurance. It is best to train in circuits using a rather high number of repetitions and taking no rest breaks between exercises and circuits.

BEGINNER PROGRAM

Train 1 or 2 times weekly. Do 3 to 6 circuits.

1 Straight-arm pull-down and asynchronous arm movement: 20 to 25 reps per arm
2 Twisting sit-up: 20 to 30 reps on each side
3 Bent-over lateral raise: 20 to 25 reps

4 Row: 20 to 25 reps
5 Bridge (hip thrust): 20 to 30 reps

ADVANCED PROGRAM

Train at least twice weekly. Do 3 or 4 circuits.

1 Straight-arm pull-down and asynchronous arm movement: 20 to 25 reps per arm
2 Twisting sit-up: 20 to 30 reps on each side
3 Bent-over lateral raise: 20 to 25 reps
4 Row: 20 to 25 reps
5 Bridge (hip thrust): 20 to 30 reps
6 Internal shoulder rotation: 20 to 30 reps per side
7 External shoulder rotation: 20 to 30 reps per side
8 GHR: 20 to 30 reps

BACKSTROKE

■ PRIMARY MUSCLE GROUPS WORKED

The backstroke works the upper body intensely, and the muscles in the lower body are primarily working via the hip extensor muscles. The backstroke also requires powerful torso rotation and good core support.

■ ZONES TO STRENGTHEN TO PREVENT INJURIES

The most frequent injuries occur in the shoulders.

■ NECESSARY MUSCLE QUALITIES

The backstroke requires strength and endurance. It is best to train in circuits using a rather high number of repetitions and taking no rest breaks.

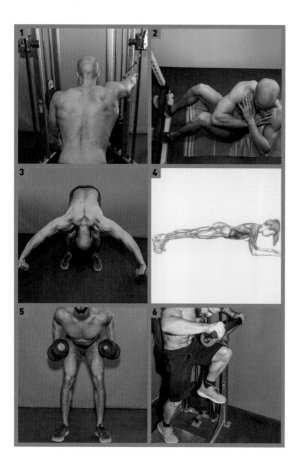

BEGINNER PROGRAM

Train 1 or 2 times weekly. Do 3 to 6 circuits.

1 Straight-arm pull-down and asynchronous arm movement: 20 to 25 reps per arm
2 Twisting sit-up: 20 to 30 reps on each side
3 Bent-over lateral raise: 20 to 25 reps
4 Plank: at least 1 minute
5 Row: 20 to 25 reps
6 Bent-knee leg lift, standing: 20 to 30 reps per leg

ADVANCED PROGRAM

Train at least twice weekly. Do 3 or 4 circuits.

1 Straight-arm pull-down and asynchronous arm movement: 20 to 25 reps per arm

2 Twisting sit-up: 20 to 30 reps on each side

3 Lateral raise lifting the arms as high as possible in an asynchronous movement: 20 to 25 reps

4 Plank: at least 2 minutes

5 Row: 20 to 25 reps

6 Bent-knee leg lift, standing: 20 to 30 reps per leg

7 Internal shoulder rotation: 20 to 30 reps per side

8 External shoulder rotation: 20 to 30 reps per side

BUTTERFLY

■ PRIMARY MUSCLE GROUPS WORKED

The butterfly provides intense work for the upper body, and the muscles in the lower body are primarily working via the hip extensor muscles.

■ ZONES TO STRENGTHEN TO PREVENT INJURIES

The most frequent injuries occur in the shoulders.

■ NECESSARY MUSCLE QUALITIES

The butterfly requires strength and endurance. It is best to train in circuits using a rather high number of repetitions and taking no rest breaks between exercises and circuits.

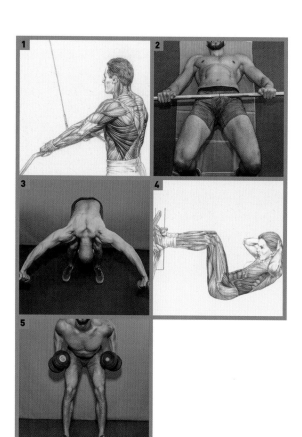

BEGINNER PROGRAM

Train 1 or 2 times weekly. Do 3 to 6 circuits.

1 Straight-arm pull-down and synchronized arms:
40 to 50 reps per arm
2 Bridge (hip thrust):
20 to 40 reps
3 Bent-over lateral raise:
20 to 25 reps
4 Sit-up: 20 to 30 reps
5 Row: 20 to 25 reps

ADVANCED PROGRAM

Train at least twice weekly. Do 3 or 4 circuits.

1 Straight-arm pull-down
and synchronized arms:
40 to 50 reps per arm
2 Bridge (hip thrust):
20 to 40 reps
3 Bent-over lateral raise:
20 to 25 reps
4 Sit-up: 20 to 30 reps
5 Row: 20 to 25 reps
6 Internal shoulder rotation: 20 to 30 reps
per side
7 External shoulder rotation: 20 to 30 reps
per side
8 GHR: 20 to 30 reps

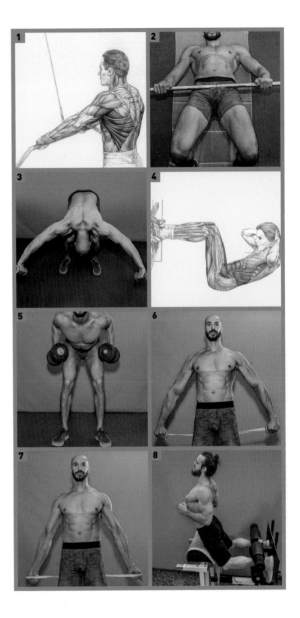

■ PRIMARY MUSCLE GROUPS WORKED

The breaststroke provides intense work for the upper body, and the muscles in the lower body are primarily working via the hip flexor and extensor muscles and the abductors.

■ ZONES TO STRENGTHEN TO PREVENT INJURIES

The most frequent injuries occur in the shoulders and the hip rotators.

■ NECESSARY MUSCLE QUALITIES

The breaststroke requires strength and endurance. It is best to train in circuits using a rather high number of repetitions and taking no rest breaks between exercises and circuits.

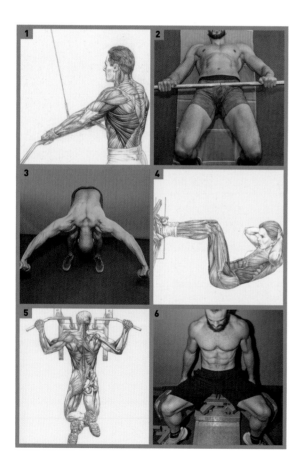

BEGINNER PROGRAM

Train 1 or 2 times weekly. Do 3 to 6 circuits.

1 Straight-arm pull-down and synchronized arms:
40 to 50 reps per arm
2 Bridge (hip thrust):
20 to 30 reps
3 Bent-over lateral raise:
20 to 25 reps
4 Sit-up: 20 to 30 reps
5 Pull-up: 20 to 25 reps
6 Hip abduction: 20 to 30 reps

ADVANCED PROGRAM

Train at least twice weekly. Do 3 or 4 circuits.

1 Straight-arm pull-down and synchronized arms:
40 to 50 reps per arm
2 Bridge (hip thrust):
20 to 30 reps
3 Bent-over lateral raise:
20 to 25 reps
4 Sit-up: 20 to 30 reps
5 Pull-up: 20 to 25 reps
6 Hip abduction:
20 to 30 reps
7 Internal shoulder rotation: 20 to 30 reps per side
8 External shoulder rotation: 20 to 30 reps per side
9 GHR: 20 to 30 reps

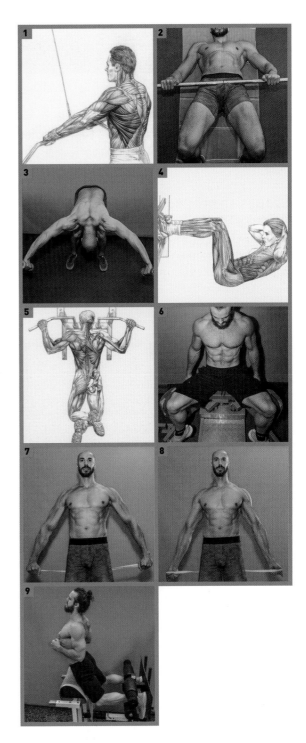

■ PRIMARY MUSCLE GROUPS WORKED

Divers work the lower part of their bodies intensely; the arm muscles work via the shoulders.

■ ZONES TO STRENGTHEN TO PREVENT INJURIES

The most frequent injuries occur in the shoulders, the hips, the knees, and the ankles.

■ NECESSARY MUSCLE QUALITIES

Divers require explosiveness. It is best to train in very short, normal sets, taking your time between sets and exercises (about 1 minute of rest) so that you can retain as much explosive power as possible.

BEGINNER PROGRAM

Train 1 or 2 times weekly.
1 Squat with a trap bar or with dumbbells: 4 sets of 8 to 12 reps
2 Sit-up: 4 sets of 10 to 20 reps
3 Plank: 3 sets held for at least 1 minute each
4 Standing calf raise: 3 sets of 8 to 12 reps

ADVANCED PROGRAM

Train at least twice weekly.
1 Squat with a trap bar or with dumbbells:
4 sets of 8 to 12 reps
2 Sit-up: 4 sets of 10 to 20 reps
3 Plank:
2 sets, held for at least 2 minutes each
4 Pull-up: 3 sets of 8 to 12 reps
5 Standing calf raise:
4 sets of 8 to 12 reps
6 GHR: 3 sets of 20 to 30 reps

WATER POLO

■ PRIMARY MUSCLE GROUPS WORKED

Water polo provides intense work for the upper part of the body; the muscles in the lower body work primarily via the hip flexors and extensors.

■ ZONES TO STRENGTHEN TO PREVENT INJURIES

The most frequent injuries occur in the shoulders, the torso rotator muscles, the back, and the hip rotator muscles.

■ NECESSARY MUSCLE QUALITIES

Water polo requires explosiveness and endurance. It is best to train in circuits, using an average number of reps and taking a few dozen seconds to rest between exercises and circuits.

BEGINNER PROGRAM

Train 1 or 2 times weekly. Do 3 to 6 circuits.

1 Ring fly: 6 to 10 reps
2 Internal shoulder rotation: 20 to 30 reps per side
3 External shoulder rotation: 20 to 30 reps per side
4 Bridge (hip thrust):
20 to 30 reps
5 Sit-up: 20 to 30 reps
6 Pull-up: 20 to 25 reps

ADVANCED PROGRAM

Train at least twice weekly. Do 3 or 4 circuits.

1 Ring fly: 6 to 10 reps
2 Internal shoulder rotation: 20 to 30 reps per side
3 External shoulder rotation: 20 to 30 reps per side
4 Bridge (hip thrust):
20 to 30 reps
5 Bent-over lateral raise:
10 to 15 reps
6 Sit-up: 20 to 30 reps
7 Pull-up: 20 to 25 reps
8 GHR: 20 to 30 reps

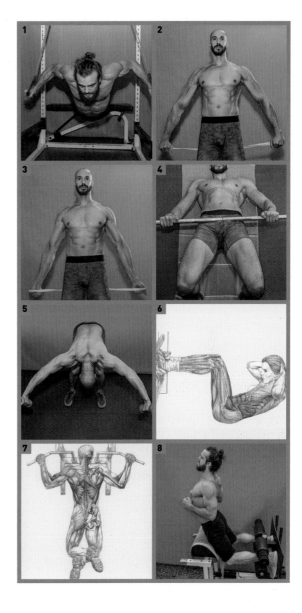

ROWING

■ PRIMARY MUSCLE GROUPS WORKED

Rowing works the upper part of the body, along with the back and biceps, just as much as it does the lower body with the legs.

■ ZONES TO STRENGTHEN TO PREVENT INJURIES

The most frequent injuries occur in the back, the shoulders, and the knees. If it is necessary because of pain or weakness, you can also do specific strengthening exercises for the forearms to bring them up to par. As a preventive measure, you should strengthen and decompress your back.

■ NECESSARY MUSCLE QUALITIES

Rowing is, above all, a strength and endurance sport. It is best to train in circuits, using a high number of reps, and to take short breaks (a few seconds) between exercises and circuits.

BEGINNER PROGRAM

Train 1 or 2 times weekly. Do 3 to 6 circuits.

1 Squat with a trap bar or with dumbbells: 20 to 30 reps
2 Row: 15 to 30 reps
3 GHR: 20 to 30 reps

ADVANCED PROGRAM

Train at least twice weekly. Do 3 or 4 circuits.

1 Squat with a trap bar or with dumbbells:
20 to 30 reps
2 Row: 15 to 30 reps
3 GHR: 20 to 30 reps
4 Reverse curl: 15 to 20 reps
5 Plank: at least 1 minute

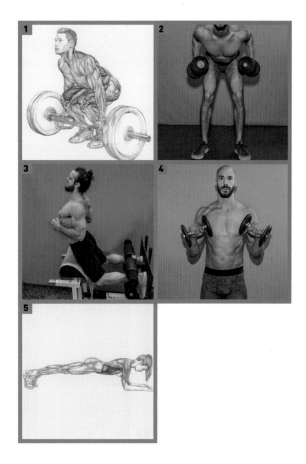

KAYAKING

■ PRIMARY MUSCLE GROUPS WORKED

Kayaking uses the upper body, involving the entire back, the shoulders, the biceps, the triceps, and the forearms. Good core strength and torso rotation are also necessary.

■ ZONES TO STRENGTHEN TO PREVENT INJURIES

The most frequent injuries occur in the back, the shoulders, and the forearms. You should strengthen and decompress your back as a preventive measure.

■ NECESSARY MUSCLE QUALITIES

Kayaking is, above all, a strength and endurance sport. It is best to train in circuits, using a high number of reps, and to take short breaks (a few seconds) between exercises and circuits.

BEGINNER PROGRAM

Train 1 or 2 times weekly. Do 3 to 6 circuits.

1 Row: 15 to 30 reps
2 GHR: 20 to 30 reps
3 Plank:
at least 1 minute
4 Twisting sit-up: 12 to 20 reps on each side

ADVANCED PROGRAM

Train at least twice weekly. Do 3 or 4 circuits.

1 Row: 15 to 30 reps
2 Standing ab twist
with a resistance band:
20 to 30 reps on each side
3 GHR: 20 to 30 reps
4 Plank:
at least 1 minute
5 Reverse curl: 15 to 20 reps
6 Twisting sit-up: 12 to 20 reps on each
side

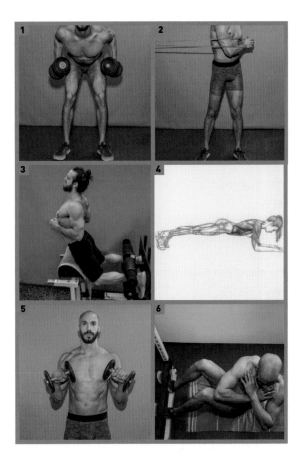

■ PRIMARY MUSCLE GROUPS WORKED

Sailing works the upper body, involving the entire back, the shoulders, the biceps, the triceps, and the forearms. Powerful thighs are required to anchor yourself correctly.

■ ZONES TO STRENGTHEN TO PREVENT INJURIES

The most frequent injuries occur in the back, the shoulders, and the forearms.

■ NECESSARY MUSCLE QUALITIES

Sailing is, above all, a strength and endurance sport. Explosive power is also required intermittently. It is best to train in circuits, using a high number of reps, and to take short breaks (a few seconds between exercises and circuits).

BEGINNER PROGRAM

Train 1 or 2 times weekly. Do 3 to 6 circuits.

1 Row: 20 to 30 reps
2 GHR: 20 to 30 reps
3 Straight-arm pull-down: 20 to 25 reps
4 Plank: at least 1 minute

ADVANCED PROGRAM

Train at least twice weekly. Do 3 or 4 circuits.

1 Row: 20 to 30 reps
2 GHR: 20 to 30 reps
3 Straight-arm pull-down:
20 to 25 reps
4 Plank:
at least 1 minute
5 Reverse curl: 15 to 20 reps
6 Squat with a trap bar or with dumbbells:
20 to 30 reps

SPECIAL NOTE

If you like sailing, surfing, or windsurfing, you probably do not enjoy spending a lot of time indoors in the gym. Your program should be as time efficient as possible and focused on the essentials. Flexibility is important: On days when the weather is bad and you cannot be outdoors doing your sport, intensive strength training can bridge the gap between two sport outings. In contrast, when you are engaging in your sport regularly, you can ease up on your strength training program.

Additionally, if you live far away from where you sail, strength training can help you best prepare to avoid debilitating muscle soreness when you start back too quickly. Your muscles will be ready so that you can give your maximum effort while minimizing the time needed to reacclimate yourself to the different movements required in your sport.

■ PRIMARY MUSCLE GROUPS WORKED

Surfing requires just as much strength in the upper body (involving the entire back, the shoulders, and the arms) as in the lower body (coming from the thighs). Because the spine serves as the link between the arms and the legs, the low back, the core, and the muscles that rotate the torso work very hard.

■ ZONES TO STRENGTHEN TO PREVENT INJURIES

The most frequent injuries occur in the shoulders, the knees, and the back. Medical examinations show that at least 50 percent of professional surfers have serious degeneration in the discs in the spine.[17] Additionally, numerous imbalances are found in the shoulders, both between the right and left sides and in the ability of the shoulders to lift the arms in the air; the ability to lift the arms is much weaker than the inverse movement.[18] These strength imbalances promote shoulder injuries, and they should be corrected through strength training. If necessary, because of pain or weakness, specific strength training for the forearms could also be planned.

■ NECESSARY MUSCLE QUALITIES

Surfing is, above all, an endurance sport. Explosive power is also required intermittently. It is best to train in circuits, using a high number of reps with short rest breaks (a few seconds) between exercises and circuits.

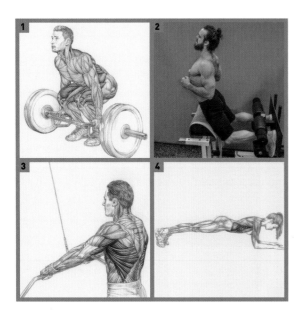

BEGINNER PROGRAM

Train 1 or 2 times weekly. Do 3 to 6 circuits.

1 Squat with a trap bar or with dumbbells: 20 to 30 reps
2 GHR: 20 to 30 reps
3 Straight-arm pull-down: 20 to 25 reps
4 Plank: at least 1 minute

ADVANCED PROGRAM

Train at least twice weekly. Do 3 or 4 circuits.

1 Squat with a trap bar or with dumbbells:
20 to 30 reps
2 GHR: 20 to 30 reps
3 Straight-arm pull-down:
20 to 25 reps
4 Plank:
at least 1 minute
5 Squat with a trap bar or with dumbbells:
20 to 30 reps
6 Twisting sit-up: 12 to 20 reps on each side

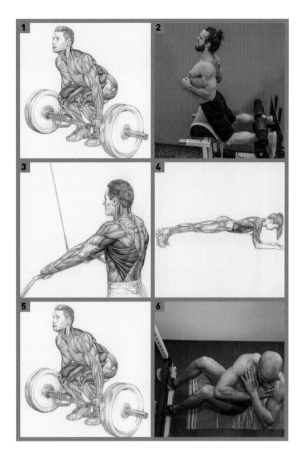

WINDSURFING

■ PRIMARY MUSCLE GROUPS WORKED

Windsurfing requires balance from all the muscles in the body as well as resistance from the back, the arms, the forearms, and the thighs. All the core muscles are heavily used.

■ ZONES TO STRENGTHEN TO PREVENT INJURIES

The most frequent injuries occur in the back, the shoulders, the forearms, the hips, the knees, and the ankles.

■ NECESSARY MUSCLE QUALITIES

Windsurfing is, above all, a sport of resistance and endurance. It is best to train in circuits, using a high number of reps with short rest breaks (a few seconds) between exercises and circuits.

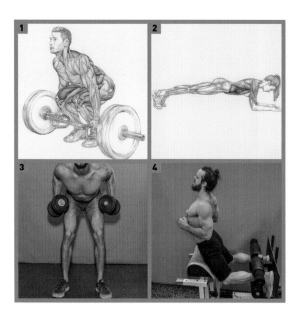

BEGINNER PROGRAM

Train 1 or 2 times weekly. Do 3 to 6 circuits.

1 Squat with a trap bar or with dumbbells: 20 to 30 reps
2 Plank:
at least 1 minute
3 Row: 20 to 30 reps
4 GHR: 20 to 30 reps

ADVANCED PROGRAM

Train at least twice weekly. Do 3 or 4 circuits.

1 Squat with a trap bar or with dumbbells:
20 to 30 reps
2 Sit-up: 12 to 20 reps
3 Row: 20 to 30 reps
4 GHR: 20 to 30 reps
5 Plank:
at least 2 minutes
6 Reverse curl: 15 to 20 reps

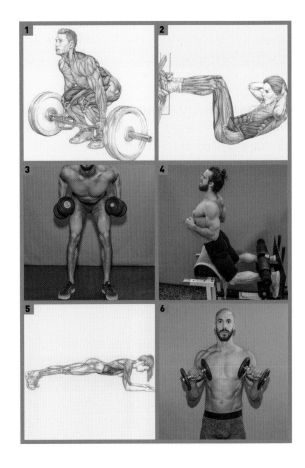

WATER SKIING

■ PRIMARY MUSCLE GROUPS WORKED

Water skiing requires counterbalance from all the muscles in the body as well as resistance from the back, the arms, the forearms, and the thighs.

■ ZONES TO STRENGTHEN TO PREVENT INJURIES

The most frequent injuries occur in the back, the shoulders, the forearms, the hips, the knees, and the ankles.

■ NECESSARY MUSCLE QUALITIES

Water skiing is, above all, a sport of resistance and endurance. It is best to train in circuits, using a high number of reps with short rest breaks (a few seconds) between exercises and circuits.

BEGINNER PROGRAM

Train 1 or 2 times weekly. Do 3 to 6 circuits.

1 Row: 20 to 30 reps
2 GHR: 20 to 30 reps
3 Squat with a trap bar or with dumbbells: 20 to 30 reps
4 Plank: at least 1 minute

ADVANCED PROGRAM

Train at least twice weekly. Do 3 or 4 circuits.

1 Row: 20 to 30 reps
2 GHR: 20 to 30 reps
3 Plank:
at least 1 minute
4 Reverse curl: 15 to 20 reps
5 Squat with a trap bar or with dumbbells:
20 to 30 reps
6 Twisting sit-up: 12 to 20 reps on each
side

TRAINING PROGRAMS FOR RACQUET OR THROWING SPORTS

RACQUET SPORTS

■ PRIMARY MUSCLE GROUPS WORKED

Racquet sports (e.g., tennis, table tennis, badminton, squash) work the lower body as well as the upper body. They require powerful torso rotation as well as serious arm work via the shoulders and back.

The arms transmit force, but that force is coming from the rest of the body. Thus, strength in the thighs and the trunk provides more than half of the power in a serve.[19] Tennis players with the most powerful serves are those who can mobilize more strength in the trunk because they have a larger range of motion to twist than average players.[19] You should focus on strengthening the muscles that allow you to rotate your torso.

■ ZONES TO STRENGTHEN TO PREVENT INJURIES

The most frequent injuries occur in the back, especially the low back. In the long term, these are the main weak points for tennis players.[20] Then there are injuries to the shoulders, knees, hips, and forearms, as well as tears in the abdominal muscles, adductors, and Achilles' tendons.

■ NECESSARY MUSCLE QUALITIES

Racquet sports are activities involving both explosiveness and endurance. It is best to train in circuits, using an average number of reps with short rest breaks (a few dozen seconds between exercises and about 1 minute between circuits).

BEGINNER PROGRAM

Train 1 or 2 times weekly. Do 3 to 6 circuits.

1 Side lunge: 15 to 20 reps
per leg
2 Combo twist, with simultaneous pushing
and pulling: 15 to 20 reps per side
3 Standing calf raise:
30 to 50 reps
4 Finger extension:
20 to 30 reps per hand
5 Twisting sit-up: 12 to 20 reps on each
side

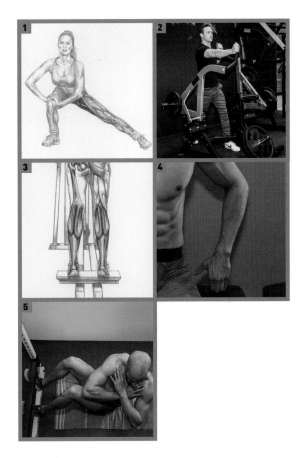

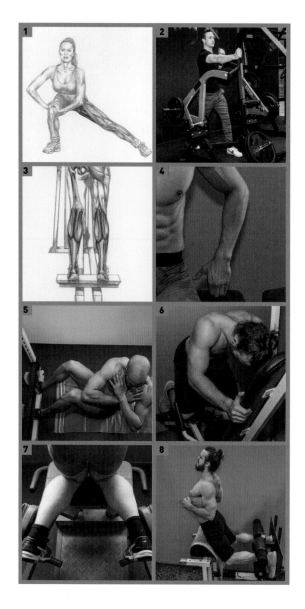

ADVANCED PROGRAM

Train at least twice weekly. Do 3 or 4 circuits.

1 Side lunge:
15 to 20 reps per leg
2 Combo twist, with simultaneous pushing and pulling: 15 to 20 reps per side
3 Standing calf raise:
30 to 50 reps
4 Finger extension:
20 to 30 reps per hand
5 Twisting sit-up: 12 to 20 reps on each side
6 External hip rotation:
20 to 30 reps
7 Internal hip rotation:
20 to 30 reps
8 GHR: 20 to 30 reps

DISCUS THROW

■ PRIMARY MUSCLE GROUPS WORKED

The discus throw works the muscles in the lower body, the torso rotator muscles, and the core, which have to transmit all their power to the arm via the shoulder and the pectoralis major.

■ ZONES TO STRENGTHEN TO PREVENT INJURIES

The most frequent injuries occur in the shoulder, the lower back, the torso rotator muscles, and the hips, as well as the knees and ankles. The tendon of the long head of the biceps is under a lot of tension as it stretches, so tendinitis and tears are frequent. Warm up the tendon well with several sets of front raises in sets of 20 to 30 reps before any kind of workout.

■ NECESSARY MUSCLE QUALITIES

The discus throw requires explosiveness. It is best to train in very short, normal sets of 4 to 12 reps. Rest for a few minutes between exercises.

BEGINNER PROGRAM

Train 1 or 2 times weekly.
1 Ab twist, lying down, with bent legs:
4 sets of 6 to 10 reps
on each side
2 Squat with a trap bar or with dumbbells:
4 sets of 4 to 8 reps
3 Standing ab twist with a side twist
using a resistance band attached to
a high point: 3 sets of 8 to 12 reps
on each side
4 Ring fly: 4 sets of 10 to 12 reps
5 Standing calf raise: 5 sets of 10 to 12 reps

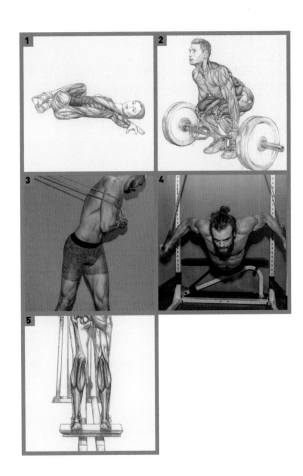

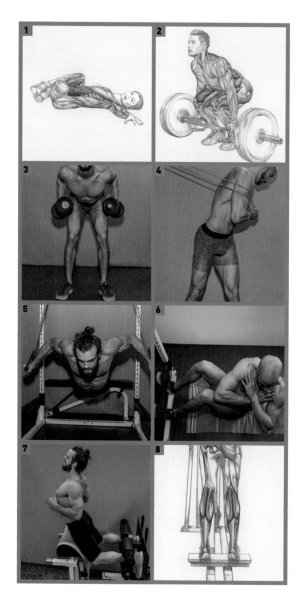

ADVANCED PROGRAM

Train at least twice weekly.
1 Ab twist, lying down, with bent legs:
4 sets of 6 to 10 reps
on each side
2 Squat with a trap bar or with dumbbells:
4 sets of 4 to 8 reps
3 Row: 4 sets of 10 to 12 reps
4 Standing ab twist with a side twist
using a resistance band attached to
a high point: 3 sets of 8 to 12 reps
on each side
5 Ring fly: 4 sets of 10 to 12 reps
6 Twisting sit-up: 4 sets of 10 to 12 reps on
each side
7 GHR: 4 sets of 10 to 12 reps
8 Standing calf raise: 5 sets of 10 to 12 reps

HAMMER THROW

■ PRIMARY MUSCLE GROUPS WORKED

The hammer throw provides intense work for the lower body, the torso rotator muscles, and the hips, as well as the core. These muscles have to transmit all their power to the arms.

■ ZONES TO STRENGTHEN TO PREVENT INJURIES

The most frequent injuries occur in the upper and lower back, the shoulders, and the torso and hip rotator muscles, as well as the knees and ankles.

■ NECESSARY MUSCLE QUALITIES

The hammer throw requires explosiveness. It is best to train in very short, normal sets of 4 to 12 reps. Rest for a few minutes between exercises.

BEGINNER PROGRAM

Train 1 or 2 times weekly.
1 Ab twist, lying down, with bent legs:
4 sets of 6 to 10 reps
on each side
2 Squat with a trap bar or with dumbbells:
4 sets of 4 to 8 reps
3 Standing ab twist with a side twist
using a resistance band attached to
a high point: 3 sets of 8 to 12 reps
on each side
4 Row: 4 sets of 10 to 12 reps
5 Twisting sit-up: 4 sets of 10 to 12 reps on each side
6 Standing calf raise: 5 sets of 10 to 12 reps

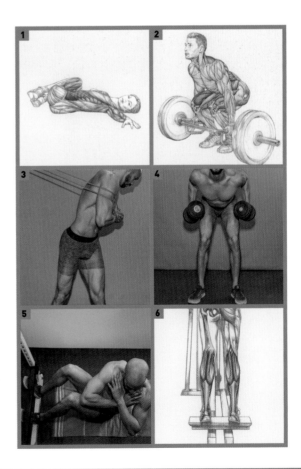

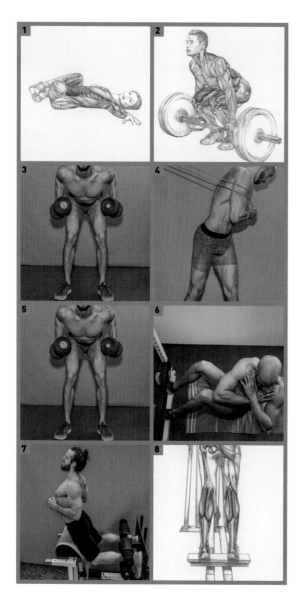

ADVANCED PROGRAM

Train at least twice weekly.
1 Ab twist, lying down, with bent legs:
4 sets of 6 to 10 reps
on each side
2 Squat with a trap bar or with dumbbells:
4 sets of 4 to 8 reps
3 Row: 4 sets of 10 to 12 reps
4 Standing ab twist with a side twist
using a resistance band attached to
a high point: 3 sets of 8 to 12 reps
on each side
5 Row: 4 sets of 10 to 12 reps
6 Twisting sit-up: 4 sets of 10 to 12 reps on
each side
7 GHR: 4 sets of 10 to 12 reps
8 Standing calf raise: 5 sets of 10 to 12 reps

JAVELIN THROW

■ PRIMARY MUSCLE GROUPS WORKED

The javelin throw provides intense work for the lower body and the hip and torso rotator muscles, as well as the core. These muscles have to transmit all their power to the arm via the shoulder and the pectoralis major.

■ ZONES TO STRENGTHEN TO PREVENT INJURIES

The most frequent injuries occur in the upper and lower back, the shoulder, the elbow, the wrist, the torso rotator muscles, and the hips, as well as the knees and ankles. The tendon of the long head of the biceps is under a lot of tension as it stretches, so tendinitis, and even tears, are frequent. Warm up the tendon well with several sets of front raises in sets of 20 to 30 reps before any kind of workout.

■ NECESSARY MUSCLE QUALITIES

The javelin throw requires explosiveness. It is best to train in very short, normal sets of 4 to 12 reps. Rest for a few minutes between exercises.

BEGINNER PROGRAM

Train 1 or 2 times weekly.
1 Lunge: 4 sets of 4 to 8 reps per leg
2 Standing ab twist with a side twist using a resistance band attached to a high point: 3 sets of 8 to 12 reps on each side
3 Ring fly: 4 sets of 4 to 8 reps
4 Standing calf raise: 5 sets of 10 to 12 reps
5 Internal shoulder rotation: 4 sets of 12 reps per side

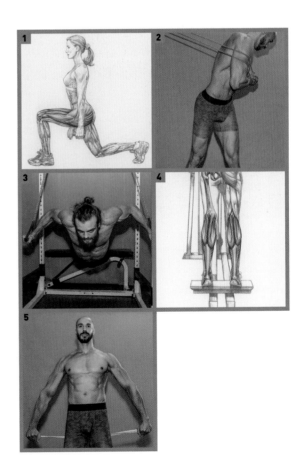

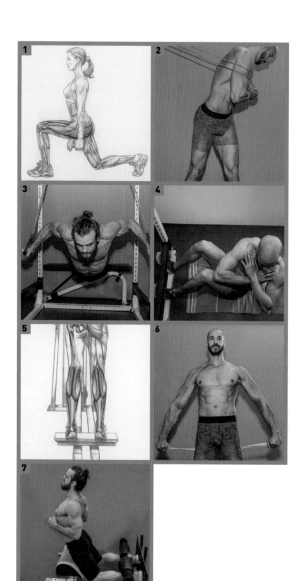

ADVANCED PROGRAM

Train at least twice weekly.
1 Lunge: 4 sets of 4 to 8 reps per leg
2 Standing ab twist with a side twist using a resistance band attached to a high point: 3 sets of 8 to 12 reps on each side
3 Ring fly: 4 sets of 4 to 8 reps
4 Twisting sit-up: 4 sets of 10 to 12 reps on each side
5 Standing calf raise: 5 sets of 10 to 12 reps
6 Internal shoulder rotation: 4 sets of 12 reps per side
7 GHR: 4 sets of 10 to 12 reps

SHOT PUT

■ PRIMARY MUSCLE GROUPS WORKED

The shot put provides intense work for the muscles in the upper and lower body.

■ ZONES TO STRENGTHEN TO PREVENT INJURIES

The most frequent injuries occur in the upper and lower back, the shoulder, the elbow, the wrist, the torso rotator muscles, and the hips, as well as the knees and ankles. Shot putters typically have an imbal-ance between the shoulder muscles that project the arm forward and those that bring it backward. Since the latter muscles are not used as often, they are usually weaker, and this is a factor in injuries.[21]

■ NECESSARY MUSCLE QUALITIES

The shot put requires explosiveness. It is best to train in very short, normal sets of 4 to 12 reps. Rest for a few minutes between exercises.

BEGINNER PROGRAM

Train 1 or 2 times weekly.
1 Lunge: 4 sets of 4 to 8 reps per leg
2 Standing ab twist with a side twist using a resistance band attached to a midlevel point: 3 sets of 8 to 12 reps on each side
3 Jammer press: 4 sets of 4 to 8 reps
4 Standing calf raise: 5 sets of 10 to 12 reps
5 GHR: 4 sets of 10 to 12 reps

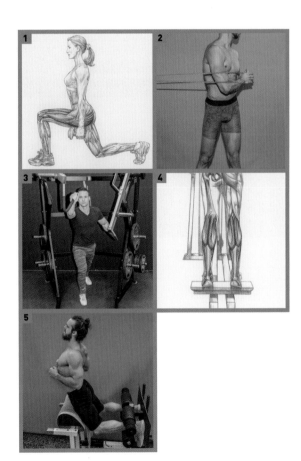

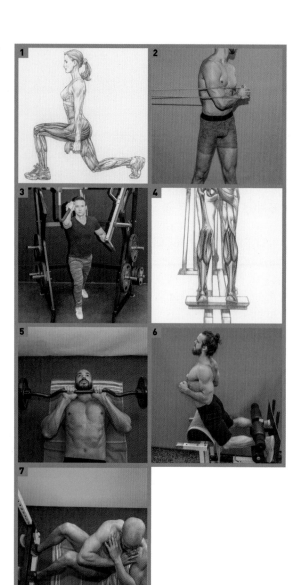

ADVANCED PROGRAM

Train at least twice weekly.
1 Lunge: 4 sets of 4 to 8 reps
per leg
2 Standing ab twist with a side twist
using a resistance band attached to
a midlevel point: 3 sets of 8 to 12 reps
on each side
3 Jammer press: 4 sets
of 4 to 8 reps
4 Standing calf raise: 5 sets
of 10 to 12 reps
5 JM press: 4 sets of 4 to 8 reps
6 GHR: 4 sets of 10 to 12 reps
7 Twisting sit-up: 4 sets of 10 to 12 reps on
each side

PETANQUE AND BOWLING

■ PRIMARY MUSCLE GROUPS WORKED

These sports in which you project something with your arm down low require just as much upper-body work (via serious work in the shoulder and the forearms) as core and the leg work. The lumbar muscles are strongly mobilized, especially because of the torso learning forward.

■ ZONES TO STRENGTHEN TO PREVENT INJURIES

The most frequent injuries occur in the back and the shoulders. If necessary, because of pain or weakness, specific strength training for the forearms could also be planned. As a preventive measure, you should also strengthen and decompress the low back.

■ NECESSARY MUSCLE QUALITIES

These are, above all, explosive sports, but players are engaged for a long period of time, which also means that endurance plays a role. So it is best to train in circuits, using a rather low number of reps with short rest breaks (a few dozen seconds) between exercises and circuits.

BEGINNER PROGRAM

Train 1 or 2 times weekly. Do 3 to 6 circuits.

1 Front raise:
6 to 12 reps
2 Row: 15 to 20 reps
3 Lunge: 6 to 8 reps per leg
4 GHR: 20 to 30 reps

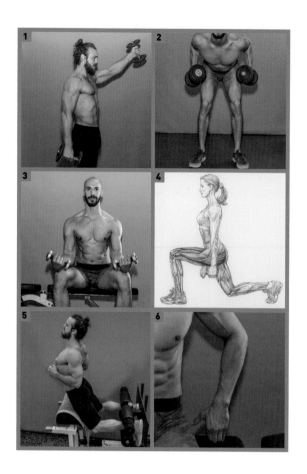

ADVANCED PROGRAM

Train at least twice weekly. Do 3 or 4 circuits.

1 Front raise:
6 to 12 reps
2 Row: 15 to 20 reps
3 Wrist curl: 20 to 30 reps
4 Lunge: 6 to 8 reps per leg
5 GHR: 20 to 30 reps
6 Finger extension: 20 to 30 reps

BASEBALL AND SOFTBALL

■ PRIMARY MUSCLE GROUPS WORKED
Baseball and softball use upper- and lower-body muscles, but the degree to which they are used varies depending on the player's position.

■ ZONES TO STRENGTHEN TO PREVENT INJURIES
The most frequent injuries occur in the upper and lower back, the shoulder, the elbow, the wrist, and the torso and hip rotator muscles, as well as the knees and ankles.

■ NECESSARY MUSCLE QUALITIES
Baseball and softball require both explosiveness and endurance. It is best to train in short, normal sets. Take a 1-minute rest break between sets and exercises.

BEGINNER PROGRAM

Train 1 or 2 times weekly.
1 Lunge: 4 sets of 4 to 8 reps per leg
2 Standing ab twist with a resistance band: 3 sets of 12 to 15 reps on each side
3 Row: 4 sets of 8 to 12 reps
4 GHR: 4 sets of 12 to 15 reps

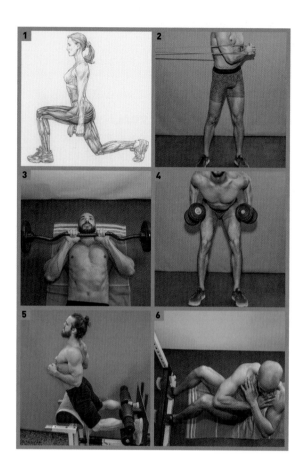

ADVANCED PROGRAM

Train at least twice weekly.
1 Lunge: 4 sets of 8 to 12 reps
per leg
2 Standing ab twist
with a resistance band:
3 sets of 12 to 15 reps
on each side
3 JM press: 4 sets of 8 to 12 reps
4 Row: 4 sets of 8 to 12 reps
5 GHR: 4 sets of 12 to 15 reps
6 Twisting sit-up: 4 sets of 12 to 15 reps on
each side

TRAINING PROGRAMS FOR CYCLING AND ROAD SPORTS

ROAD CYCLING

■ PRIMARY MUSCLE GROUPS WORKED

Cycling works the lower body intensely, including the glutes, the thighs, and the calves. The spine, the core muscles, and the arms are also strongly mobilized to ensure the cyclist's balance.

■ ZONES TO STRENGTHEN TO PREVENT INJURIES

The most frequent injuries occur in the back, the hips, the knees, and the ankles.

■ NECESSARY MUSCLE QUALITIES

Road cycling is, above all, an endurance sport. It is best to train in circuits, using a rather high number of reps and with short rest breaks (a few seconds) between exercises and circuits.

BEGINNER PROGRAM

Train 1 or 2 times weekly. Do 2 to 5 circuits.

1 Squat with a trap bar or with dumbbells: 20 to 35 reps
2 GHR: 20 to 30 reps
3 Bent-knee leg lift, seated: 20 to 30 reps per leg
4 Crouching calf raise: 30 to 50 reps

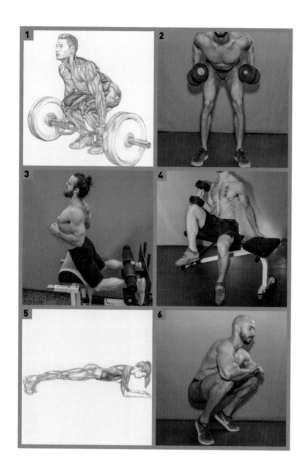

ADVANCED PROGRAM

Train at least twice weekly. Do 2 to 4 circuits.

1 Squat with a trap bar or with dumbbells:
20 to 35 reps
2 Row: 20 to 30 reps
3 GHR: 20 to 30 reps
4 Bent-knee leg lift, seated: 20 to 30 reps
per leg
5 Plank:
at least 1 minute
6 Crouching calf raise: 30 to 50 reps

TRACK CYCLING

■ PRIMARY MUSCLE GROUPS WORKED

Cycling provides intense work for the lower body, including the glutes, the thighs, and the calves. The spine, the core muscles, and the arms are also strongly mobilized to ensure the cyclist's balance.

■ ZONES TO STRENGTHEN TO PREVENT INJURIES

The most frequent injuries occur in the back, the hips, the knees, and the ankles.

■ NECESSARY MUSCLE QUALITIES

Track cycling is, above all, a sport that requires explosiveness. It is best to train in circuits, using very few reps and with short rest breaks (a few dozen seconds) between exercises and circuits.

BEGINNER PROGRAM

Train 1 or 2 times weekly. Do 2 to 5 circuits.

1 Squat with a trap bar or with dumbbells: 8 to 12 reps
2 GHR: 20 to 30 reps
3 Bent-knee leg lift, seated: 12 to 20 reps per leg
4 Crouching calf raise: 20 to 30 reps

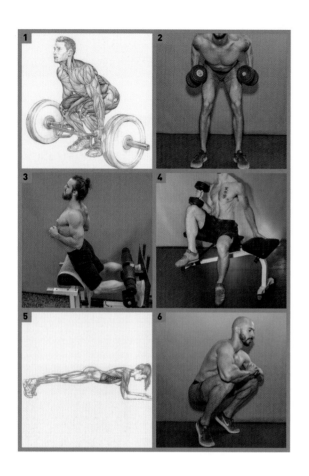

ADVANCED PROGRAM

Train at least twice weekly. Do 2 to 4 circuits.

1 Squat with a trap bar or with dumbbells:
8 to 12 reps
2 Row: 12 to 20 reps
3 GHR: 20 to 30 reps
4 Bent-knee leg lift, seated: 12 to 20 reps
per leg
5 Plank:
at least 1 minute
6 Crouching calf raise: 20 to 30 reps

ALL-TERRAIN AND BMX CYCLING

■ PRIMARY MUSCLE GROUPS WORKED

Cycling works the lower body intensely, including the glutes, the thighs, and the calves. The spine, the core muscles, and the arms are also strongly mobilized to ensure the cyclist's balance.

■ ZONES TO STRENGTHEN TO PREVENT INJURIES

The most frequent injuries occur in the back, the hips, the knees, and the ankles.

■ NECESSARY MUSCLE QUALITIES

All-terrain and BMX are, above all, endurance sports. The primary goal of strength training is to ensure the braking power of the thighs. It is best to train in circuits, using a rather high number of reps, and take short rest breaks (a few seconds) between exercises and circuits.

BEGINNER PROGRAM

Train 1 or 2 times weekly. Do 2 to 5 circuits.

1 Squat with a trap bar or with dumbbells:
30 to 50 reps
2 JM press: 12 to 25 reps
3 GHR: 20 to 30 reps
4 Standing calf raise: 30 to 50 reps

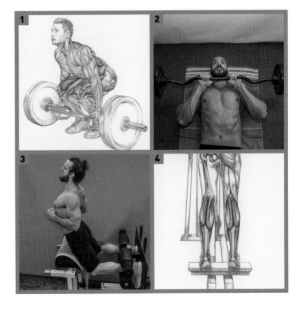

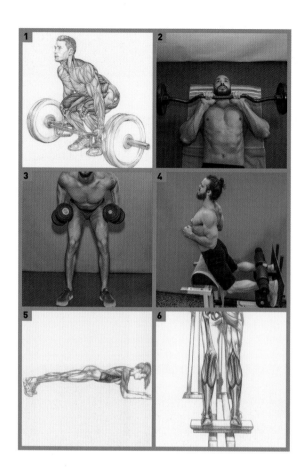

ADVANCED PROGRAM

Train at least twice weekly. Do 2 to 4 circuits without resting.

1 Squat with a trap bar or with dumbbells: 30 to 50 reps
2 JM press: 12 to 25 reps
3 Row: 12 to 20 reps
4 GHR: 20 to 30 reps
5 Plank:
at least 1 minute
6 Standing calf raise: 30 to 50 reps

AUTOMOBILE SPORTS

■ **PRIMARY MUSCLE GROUPS WORKED**
Automobile sports use the upper and lower body. All of the muscles act as one to ensure total support for the driver.

■ **ZONES TO STRENGTHEN TO PREVENT INJURIES**
The most frequent injuries (other than accidents) occur in the back, the forearms, and the neck.

■ **NECESSARY MUSCLE QUALITIES**
The primary objective of strength training is to prevent pain and overuse injuries that drivers experience. It is best to train in rather long, normal sets with short rest breaks (about 30 seconds) between sets and exercises.

BEGINNER PROGRAM

Train 1 or 2 times weekly.
1 JM press: 3 sets of 10 to 15 reps
2 Shrug using an adjustable pulley: 3 sets of 20 to 30 reps
3 GHR: 4 sets of 10 to 15 reps
4 Finger flexion using a hand grip strengthener: 2 sets of 50 to 100 reps

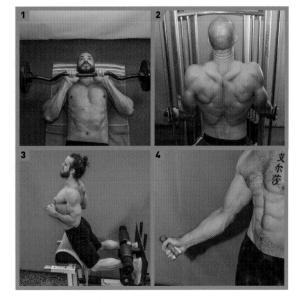

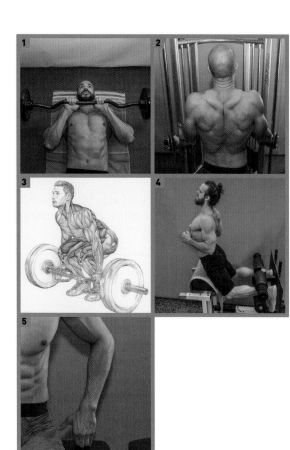

ADVANCED PROGRAM

Train at least twice weekly.
1 JM press: 3 sets of 10 to 15 reps
2 Shrug using an adjustable pulley: 3 sets of 20 to 30 reps
3 Squat with a trap bar or with dumbbells: 2 sets of 6 to 8 reps
4 GHR: 4 sets of 10 to 15 reps
5 Finger extension: 2 sets of 50 to 100 reps

■ PRIMARY MUSCLE GROUPS WORKED

Motorcycle riding works the lower body especially, but the rest of the muscles in the body are not forgotten; they must work together to ensure the rider's balance.

■ ZONES TO STRENGTHEN TO PREVENT INJURIES

The most frequent injuries (other than accidents) occur in the back, the forearms, the knees, and the neck.

■ NECESSARY MUSCLE QUALITIES

Strength training's primary purpose is to ensure the braking power of the thighs, especially in motocross. The second purpose is to prevent pain and overuse injuries that riders experience. It is best to train in rather long, normal sets with short rest breaks (30 seconds to 1 minute) after each set.

BEGINNER PROGRAM

Train 1 or 2 times weekly.
1 Squat with a trap bar or with dumbbells: 2 sets of 12 to 15 reps
2 JM press: 2 sets of 10 to 15 reps
3 GHR: 3 sets of 10 to 15 reps
4 Finger flexion using a hand grip strengthener: 2 sets of 50 to 100 reps

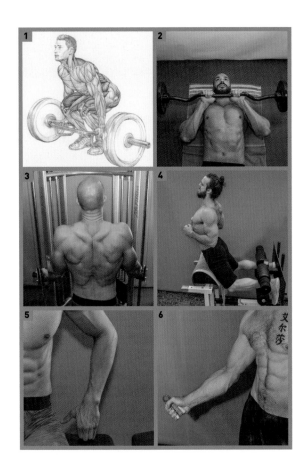

ADVANCED PROGRAM

Train at least twice weekly.
1 Squat with a trap bar or with dumbbells: 3 sets of 12 to 15 reps
2 JM press: 3 sets of 10 to 15 reps
3 Shrug using an adjustable pulley: 2 sets of 20 to 30 reps
4 GHR: 3 sets of 10 to 15 reps
5 Finger extension: 2 sets of 50 to 100 reps
6 Finger flexion using a hand grip strengthener: 2 sets of 50 to 100 reps

HORSEBACK RIDING

■ PRIMARY MUSCLE GROUPS WORKED

Horseback riding requires counterbalance from the muscles, especially the thighs. Core support should be very solid to help you maintain your balance.

■ ZONES TO STRENGTHEN TO PREVENT INJURIES

The most frequent injuries occur in the upper and lower back, the hips, the knees, and the ankles.

■ NECESSARY MUSCLE QUALITIES

Horseback riding is, above all, a sport of resistance and endurance. It is best to train in circuits, with a rather high number of reps and short rest breaks (a few seconds) between exercises and circuits.

BEGINNER PROGRAM

Train 1 or 2 times weekly. Do 3 to 5 circuits.

1 Squat with a trap bar or with dumbbells: 20 to 30 reps
2 Standing ab twist with a resistance band and the arms
in anti-rotation: 20 to 30 reps
on each side
3 Plank:
at least 1 minute
4 Standing calf raise:
20 to 30 reps
5 GHR: 20 to 30 reps

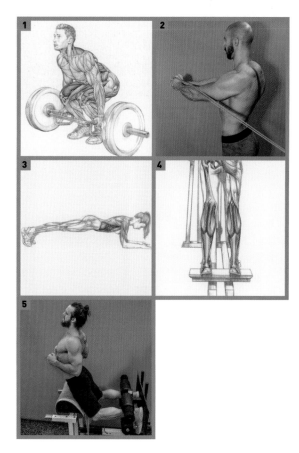

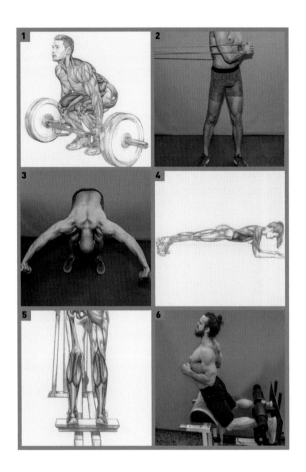

ADVANCED PROGRAM

Train at least twice weekly. Do 3 or 4 circuits.

1 Squat with a trap bar or with dumbbells:
20 to 30 reps
2 Standing ab twist with a resistance band:
20 to 30 reps
on each side
3 Bent-over lateral raise:
25 to 30 reps
4 Plank:
at least 2 minutes
5 Standing calf raise:
20 to 30 reps
6 GHR: 20 to 30 reps

TRAINING PROGRAMS FOR COMBAT SPORTS

COMBAT SPORTS

■ PRIMARY MUSCLE GROUPS WORKED

Combat sports work both the lower and upper body. They also require powerful torso rotation and a large amount of core strength.

■ ZONES TO STRENGTHEN TO PREVENT INJURIES

The most frequent injuries (other than the blows received) occur in nearly all the joints and muscles, but especially the neck, the shoulders, the back, the knees, the ankles, and the hips.

■ NECESSARY MUSCLE QUALITIES

Combat sports are explosive, strength, and endurance sports—all at the same time. It is best to train in circuits with a lower number of reps and short rest breaks (a few seconds) between exercises and circuits.

BEGINNER PROGRAM

Train 1 or 2 times weekly. Do 3 to 6 circuits.

1 Squat with a trap bar or with dumbbells:
8 to 12 reps
2 Plank:
at least 1 minute
3 Shrug using an adjustable pulley: 10 to 20 reps
4 Bent-knee leg lift, standing: 8 to 10 reps per leg

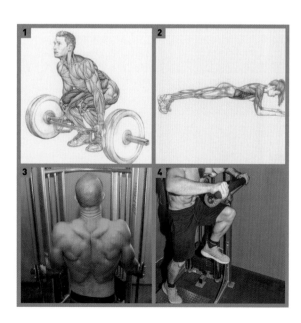

5 Combo twist, with simultaneous pulling and pushing: 15 to 20 reps per side
6 Twisting sit-up: 12 to 20 reps on each side

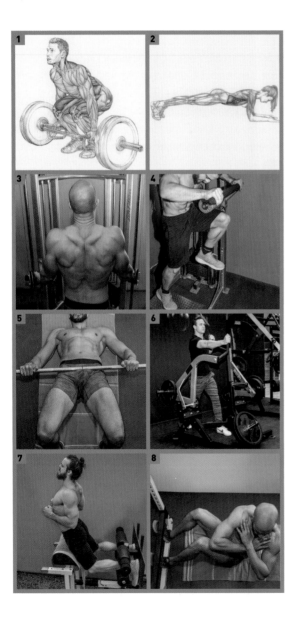

ADVANCED PROGRAM

Train at least twice weekly. Do 3 or 4 circuits.

1 Squat with a trap bar or with dumbbells: 8 to 12 reps
2 Plank:
at least 2 minutes
3 Shrug using an adjustable pulley: 10 to 20 reps
4 Bent-knee leg lift, standing: 8 to 10 reps per leg
5 Bridge (hip thrust):
10 to 15 reps
6 Combo twist, with simultaneous pulling and pushing: 15 to 20 reps per side
7 GHR: 20 to 30 reps
8 Twisting sit-up: 12 to 20 reps on each side

FENCING

■ PRIMARY MUSCLE GROUPS WORKED

Fencing provides intense work for the lower body, the arms, and the shoulder. This sport requires good core strength.

■ ZONES TO STRENGTHEN TO PREVENT INJURIES

The most frequent injuries occur in the shoulders, the back, the hip rotator muscles, the hamstrings, the knees, and the ankles.

■ NECESSARY MUSCLE QUALITIES

Fencing requires explosiveness and endurance. It is best to train in circuits using an average number of reps and to take short rest breaks (a few dozen seconds) between exercises and circuits.

BEGINNER PROGRAM

Train 1 or 2 times weekly. Do 3 to 6 circuits.

1 Lunge: 12 to 20 reps per leg
2 Front raise:
20 to 30 reps
3 Sit-up: 20 to 30 reps
4 Standing calf raise:
20 to 30 reps
5 Plank:
at least 1 minute

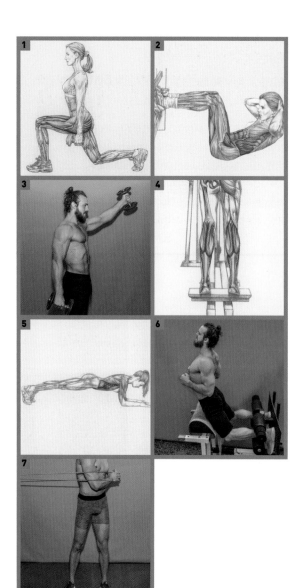

ADVANCED PROGRAM

Train at least twice weekly. Do 3 or 4 circuits.

1 Lunge: 12 to 20 reps per leg
2 Sit-up: 20 to 30 reps
3 Front raise:
20 to 30 reps
4 Standing calf raise:
20 to 30 reps
5 Plank:
at least 2 minutes
6 GHR: 20 to 30 reps
7 Standing ab twist with a resistance band:
20 to 30 reps on each side

TRAINING PROGRAMS FOR WINTER AND MOUNTAIN SPORTS

REQUIRED ACCLIMATION FOR SEASONAL SPORTS

If you live far from the area where you practice your sport—such as the ocean for surfing—or your sport is seasonal, such as skiing, strength training in advance is the best way to prepare. Following this strategy, you begin with a rather small volume of work to overcome the "aches and pains" without too much shock, and then you gradually increase the volume of work until it is a significant amount to prepare your muscles for a high level of performance. This slow progression ensures a smooth transition until you can begin your sport again.

Begin with two workouts each week, and then increase gradually until you reach one workout daily so that you match as closely as possible the effort that you are planning to demand from your body during your sport season. Use the programs provided here for each sport. At the beginning, the volume and frequency are low, and they gradually increase in power. Lastly, give yourself two or three days of rest before beginning your sport season.

PROGRAMS FOR WINTER OR SUMMER PROGRESSION WHEN ATHLETIC ACTIVITY DECREASES

During times when you cannot play your seasonal sport, take advantage of the free time to increase your strength and endurance as much as possible. When you take up your sport again, gradually decrease your volume of strength training so that all your energy is focused on your athletic activity, without losing any strength or endurance.

DOWNHILL SKIING

■ PRIMARY MUSCLE GROUPS WORKED

Downhill skiing works the lower body, of course, but it also requires good core strength and the ability to rotate the torso powerfully.

■ ZONES TO STRENGTHEN TO PREVENT INJURIES

The most frequent injuries occur in the back, the knees, the hips, and the ankles.

■ NECESSARY MUSCLE QUALITIES

Downhill skiing is, above all, a strength and endurance sport. It is best to train in circuits, with sets that are a bit longer and taking only short rest breaks (a few dozen seconds) between exercises and circuits.

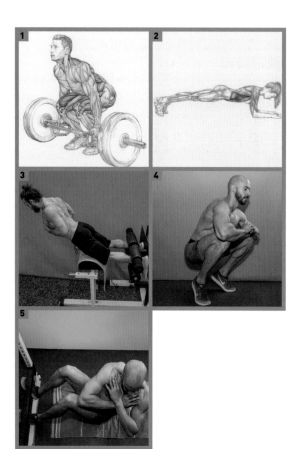

BEGINNER PROGRAM

Train 1 or 2 times weekly. Do 3 to 6 circuits.

1 Squat with a trap bar or with dumbbells:
20 to 30 reps
2 Plank:
at least 1 minute
3 Nordic hamstring curl: 20 to 30 reps
4 Crouching calf raise:
30 to 50 reps
5 Twisting sit-up: 12 to 20 reps on each side

ADVANCED PROGRAM

Train at least twice weekly. Do 3 or 4 circuits.

1 Squat with a trap bar or with dumbbells:
20 to 30 reps
2 Plank:
at least 2 minutes
3 Nordic hamstring curl: 20 to 30 reps
4 Internal hip rotation:
20 to 30 reps
5 External hip rotation:
20 to 30 reps
6 Crouching calf raise: 15 to 25 reps

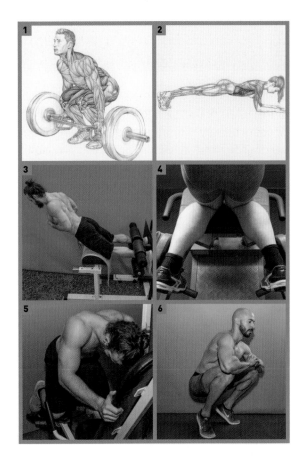

■ PRIMARY MUSCLE GROUPS WORKED

Cross-country skiing works the lower body, of course, but it also requires the ability to rotate the torso powerfully as well as serious effort from the arms via the back. Better mastery of correct posture will save you a great deal of energy. This was shown in studies comparing good cross-country skiers with beginners. Beginners' movements are less precise, so they are more complex (muscularly speaking) and use more energy.[22] Here we talk about ski economy as a benefit of strength training.

■ ZONES TO STRENGTHEN TO PREVENT INJURIES

The most frequent injuries occur in the back, the knees, the hips, and the ankles. If neces-sary, because of pain or weakness, you can devise a specific strengthening program for the forearms and the elbows to bring them up to par.

■ NECESSARY MUSCLE QUALITIES

Cross-country skiing is, above all, an endurance sport; however, it does require strength intermittently, to climb a hill, for example. It is best to train in circuits, with a rather high number of reps and taking only short rest breaks (a few seconds) between exercises and circuits.

BEGINNER PROGRAM

Train 1 or 2 times weekly. Do 3 to 6 circuits.

1 Lunge: 30 to 50 reps per leg
2 Straight-arm pulldown
and asynchronous arm movement:
20 to 25 reps per arm
3 Nordic hamstring curl: 20 to 30 reps

4 Standing calf raise:
30 to 50 reps
5 Twisting sit-up: 12 to 20 reps on each side

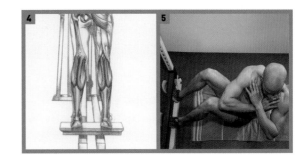

ADVANCED PROGRAM

Train at least twice weekly. Do 3 or 4 circuits.

1 Lunge: 25 to 50 reps per leg
2 Straight-arm pull-down and asynchronous arm movement: 20 to 25 reps per arm
3 Bent-knee leg lift, standing: 20 to 30 reps per leg
4 Nordic hamstring curl:
20 to 30 reps
5 Internal hip rotation:
20 to 30 reps
6 External hip rotation:
20 to 30 reps
7 Standing calf raise: 30 to 50 reps

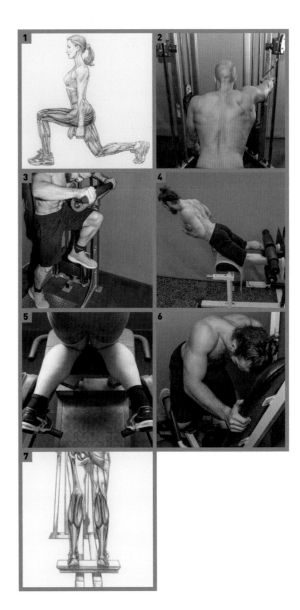

■ PRIMARY MUSCLE GROUPS WORKED

Hockey works the lower body especially, but it also requires the ability to rotate the torso powerfully as well as serious effort from the arms via the shoulders and back.

■ ZONES TO STRENGTHEN TO PREVENT INJURIES

The most frequent injuries occur in the back, the shoulders, the knees, and the hips. If necessary, because of pain or weakness, a hockey player can follow a specific streng-thening program for the forearms to bring them up to par.

■ NECESSARY MUSCLE QUALITIES

Hockey and skating are sports that require explosiveness and endurance. It is best to train in circuits, with an average number of reps, and take only short rest breaks (a few seconds) between exercises and circuits.

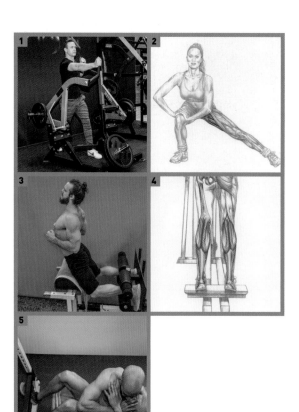

BEGINNER PROGRAM

Train 1 or 2 times weekly. Do 3 to 6 circuits.

1 Combo twist, with simultaneous pulling and pushing: 15 to 20 reps per side
2 Side lunge: 15 to 20 reps per leg
3 GHR: 20 to 30 reps
4 Standing calf raise: 30 to 50 reps
5 Twisting sit-up: 12 to 20 reps on each side

ADVANCED PROGRAM

Train at least twice weekly. Do 3 or 4 circuits.

1 Combo twist, with simultaneous pulling and pushing: 15 to 20 reps per side
2 Side lunge: 15 to 20 reps per leg
3 Bent-knee leg lift, standing: 12 to 20 reps per leg
4 GHR: 20 to 30 reps
5 Internal hip rotation: 20 to 30 reps
6 External hip rotation: 20 to 30 reps
7 Standing calf raise: 30 to 50 reps

■ PRIMARY MUSCLE GROUPS WORKED

Climbing works the entire body. More so than for any other sport, it is vital to have bulletproof forearms.

■ ZONES TO STRENGTHEN TO PREVENT INJURIES

The most frequent injuries occur in the whole back, the shoulders, the hip rotator muscles, the forearms, and the hands.

■ NECESSARY MUSCLE QUALITIES

Climbing requires strength, flexibility, and endurance. It is best to train in circuits, with an average number of sets, and to take only a few seconds to rest between exercises and circuits.

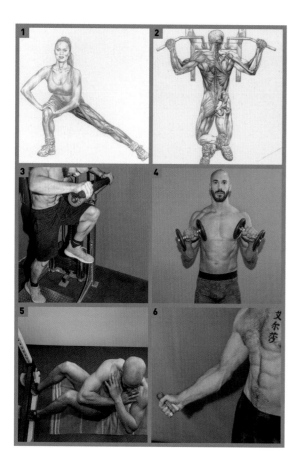

BEGINNER PROGRAM

Train 1 or 2 times weekly. Do 3 to 6 circuits.

1 Side lunge: 20 to 30 reps per leg
2 Pull-up: 20 to 40 reps
3 Bent-knee leg lift, standing, trying to go as high as possible:
20 to 30 reps per leg
4 Reverse curl: 20 to 30 reps
5 Twisting sit-up: 12 to 20 reps on each side
6 Finger flexion using a hand grip strengthener: 20 to 30 reps

ADVANCED PROGRAM

Train at least twice weekly. Do 3 or 4 circuits.

1 Side lunge: 20 to 30 reps per leg

2 Pull-up: 20 to 40 reps

3 Bent-knee leg lift, standing, trying to go as high as possible: 20 to 30 reps per leg

4 Reverse curl: 20 to 30 reps

5 GHR: 20 to 30 reps

6 Twisting sit-up: 12 to 20 reps on each side

7 Finger flexion using a hand grip strengthener: 20 to 30 reps

8 Standing calf raise: 20 to 30 reps

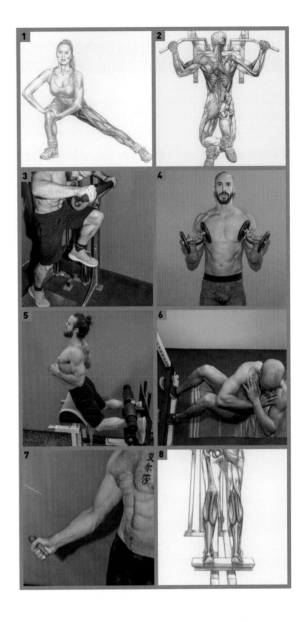

POST-TRAINING RECOVERY PROGRAMS

To ensure proper recovery after physical activity, you should use very light resistance and do certain movements numerous times to nourish the tissues that are recovering slowly due a lack of blood flow. Focus on using resistance bands since they are less traumatic for the joints than weights. And stretch only if you feel you need it.

These programs should be done at home, in the evenings after you train, and on days when you do not work out. They are very important for allowing you to work out again sooner under optimal conditions. For example, after a marathon, the position of the foot changes because of muscle fatigue. It takes more than 1 week for all the muscles to recuperate and for the foot to go back to its proper position.[23]

Strengthening the muscles will reduce these posture changes and strength training will accelerate the return to the proper position, which ultimately minimizes the risk of injury.

SHOULD YOU TRAIN IF YOU ARE STILL SORE FROM A PREVIOUS WORKOUT?

Blood flow is disturbed in muscles that are sore, or to be more precise, muscles that are damaged, and this slows down their recovery.[24] One might have expected the opposite effect, that is, an increase in blood flow that would accelerate recovery. This paradox explains, at least in part, why recovery is so slow when muscles have been worked intensely. This disturbance also temporarily decreases the performance of these aching muscles, since the muscles run out of energy faster due to a lack of oxygen. In these unfavorable conditions, recovery programs are essential.

RECOVERY PROGRAMS FOR THE UPPER BODY

Do 1 circuit with no rest breaks.
1 Internal shoulder rotation with a resistance band: 100 to 200 reps
2 External shoulder rotation with a resistance band: 100 to 200 reps
3 Myofascial massage for the extensor muscles in the forearm: at least 1 minute
4 Myofascial massage for the flexor muscles in the forearm: at least 1 minute
5 Hang from a pull-up bar (if you do not have a pull-up bar, lean forward and support yourself on the back of a bench, a chair, or the edge of a table): at least 30 seconds

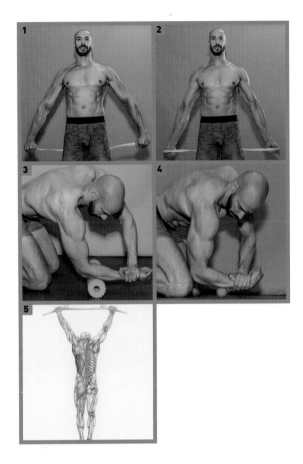

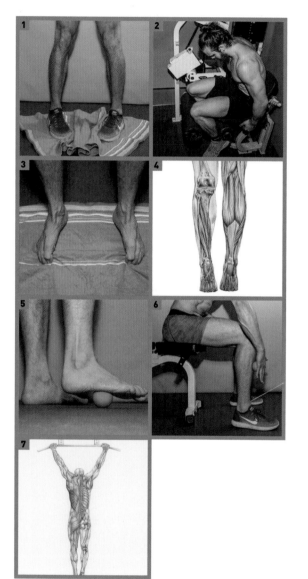

Do 1 circuit with no rest breaks.

1 Warm-up for the hip rotators using a towel (seated to make it easier if necessary): 150 to 300 reps

2 Leg curl, seated: 100 to 200 reps

3 Towel curl: 100 to 200 reps

4 Calf raise, with bare feet on the ground and no equipment: 100 to 200 reps

5 Massage for the sole of the foot with a ball: at least 1 minute per foot

6 Tibialis anterior massage: at least 1 minute per leg

7 Hang from a pull-up bar: at least 30 seconds

EXERCISE INDEX

BIBLIOGRAPHY

PART I

RUNNING SPORTS

CAN YOU SKIP STRENGTH TRAINING?

1. Seitz LB. Increases in lower-body strength transfer positively to sprint performance: a systematic review with meta-analysis. *Sports Med*, 2014. 44: 1693.

HOW CAN STRENGTH TRAINING HELP YOU RUN FASTER?

2. Pincheira PA. The repeated bout effect can occur without mechanical and neuromuscular changes after a bout of eccentric exercise. *Scand J Med Sci Sports*, May 2018.

3. Mohr M. Muscle damage, inflammatory, immune and performance responses to three football games in 1 week in competitive male players. *Eur J Appl Physiol*, 2016. 116: 179.

4. Lauersen JB. The effectiveness of exercise interventions to prevent sports injuries: a systematic review and meta-analysis of randomized controlled trials. *Br J Sports Med*, 2014. 48: 871.

5. Malone S. Can the workload–injury relationship be moderated by improved strength, speed and repeated-sprint qualities? *J Sci Med Sport*, 2018.

6. Jakobsen JR. Remodeling of muscle fibres approaching the human myotendinous junction. *Scand J Med Sci Sports*, 2018.

7. Schaefer D. Does lean mass asymmetry influence impulse and peak force asymmetry during landing in collegiate athletes. *J Strength Cond Res*, 2017. 31 (suppl. 1): S13.

8. Lieber RL. Biomechanical response of skeletal muscle to eccentric contractions. *J Sport Health Sci*, 2018.

9. Aagaard P. Spinal and supraspinal control of motor function during maximal eccentric muscle contraction: effects of resistance training. *J Sport Health Sci*, 2018.

10. Milton H. One day per week of strength training improves running biomechanics. *J Strength Cond Res*, 2017. 31 (suppl. 1): S10.

11. Maas E. Novice runners show greater changes in kinematics with fatigue compared with competitive runners. *Sports Biomech*, 2018. 17.

12. Belz J. Stress and risk for depression in competitive athletes suffering from back pain – do age and gender matter? *Eur J Sport Sci*, 2018.

13. Bodine LE. The relationship between depression symptoms, pain and athletic identity in Division II NCAA athletes at preseason. *J Athl Train*, 2018. 53 (suppl.): S198.

14. Aagaard P. Increased rate of force development and neural drive of human skeletal muscle following resistance training. *J Appl Physiol*, 2002. 93: 1318.

15. Faherty M. Changes in lower extremity musculoskeletal and neuromuscular characteristics are associated with history of lower extremity musculoskeletal injury in intercollegiate athletes. *J Athl Train*, 2018. 53 (suppl.): S125.

16. Clifton DR. Functional asymmetries and lower extremity injury: direct and indirect effects. *J Athl Train*, 2018. 53 (suppl.): S135.

17. Semrow KM. Preseason risk factors to predict lower extremity musculoskeletal injuries in college athletics. *J Athl Train*, 2018. 53 (suppl.): S131.

18. Paavolainen L. Explosive-strength training improves 5-km running time by improving running economy and muscle power. *J Appl Physiol*, 1999. 86: 1527.

19. Blagrove RC. Effects of strength training on the physiological determinants of middle- and long-distance running performance: a systematic review. *Sports Med*, 2018. 48: 1117.

20. Beattie K. The effect of strength training on performance indicators in distance runners. *J Strength Cond Res*, 2017. 31: 9.

21. Sterczala A. The effects of eight weeks of resistance training on motor unit behavior of the vastus lateralis. *J Strength Cond Res*, 2017. 31 (suppl. 1): S3.

22. Sedano S. Concurrent training in elite male runners: the influence of strength versus muscular endurance training on performance outcomes. *J Strength Cond Res*, 2013. 27: 2433.

23. Hoff J. Maximal strength training improves aerobic endurance performance. *Scand J Med Sci Sports*, 2002. 12: 288.

24. Presland JD. The effect of Nordic hamstring exercise training volume on biceps femoris long head architectural adaptation. *Scand J Med Sci Sports*, 2018. 28.

WHICH MUSCLES SHOULD YOU FOCUS ON DURING STRENGTH TRAINING?

25. Beardsley C. The increasing role of the hip extensor musculature with heavier compound lower-body movements and more explosive sport actions. *Strength Cond J*, 2014. 36: 49.

26. Macadam P. The role of arm mechanics during sprint-running: a review of the literature and practical applications. *Strength Cond J*, 2018.

27. Van Wessel T. The muscle fibre type-fibre size paradox: hypertrophy or oxidative metabolism? *Eur J Appl Physiol*, 2010. 110: 665.

28. Colyer SL. Kinetic demands of sprinting shift across the acceleration phase: novel analysis of entire force waveforms. *Scand J Med Sci Sports*, 2018. 28: 1784.

29. Abdelsattar M. Relationship between Achilles tendon stiffness and ground contact time during drop jumps. *J Sports Sci Med*, 2018. 17: 223.

30. Ueno H. Potential relationship between passive plantar flexor stiffness and running performance. *Int J Sports Med*, 2018. 39: 204.

31. Takahashi C. Potential relationship between passive plantar flexor stiffness and sprint performance in sprinters. *Phys Ther Sport*, 2018. 32: 54.

32. Hunter GR. Tendon length and joint flexibility are related to running economy. *Med Sci Sports Exerc*, 2011. 43: 1492.

33. Ueno H. Relationship between Achilles tendon length and running performance in well-trained male endurance runners. *Scand J Med Sci Sports*, 2018. 28: 446.

34. Kunimasa Y. Specific muscle-tendon architecture in elite Kenyan distance runners. *Scand J Med Sci Sports*, 2014. 24: e269.

35. Hunter GR. Muscle fiber type, Achilles tendon length, potentiation, and running economy. *J Strength Cond Res*, 2015. 29: 1302.

THESE HIDDEN MUSCLES CAN MAKE YOU RUN FASTER

36. Copaver K. The effects of psoas major and lumbar lordosis on hip flexion and sprint performance. *Res Q Exerc Sport*, 2012. 83: 160.

37. Okutani H. Morphological characteristics of the psoas major muscle of 110-m hurdlers. *J Sports Sci*, 2016. 34(suppl. 1): S39.

38. Penning L. Psoas muscle and lumbar spine stability: a concept uniting existing controversies. critical review and hypothesis. *Eur Spine J*, 2000. 9: 577.

39. Park RJ. Changes in regional activity of the psoas major and quadratus lumborum with voluntary trunk and hip tasks and different spinal curvatures in sitting. *J Orthop Sports Phys Ther*, 2013. 43: 74.

40. Regev GJ. Psoas muscle architectural design, in vivo sarcomere length range, and passive tensile properties support its role as a lumbar spine stabilizer. *Spine*, 2011. 36: E1666.

41. Hides JA. Psoas and quadratus lumborum muscle asymmetry among elite Australian Football League players. *Br J Sports Med*, 2010. 44: 563.

42. Perle JF. Electromyographic activation of quadriceps in single and multi-joint exercises. *Med Sci Sports Exerc*, 2017. 49 (5S): 192.

SPECIFIC PROBLEMS

43. Brusco CM. The effects of flexibility training on exercise induced muscle damage in young men with limited hamstrings flexibility. *Scand J Med Sci Sports*, 2018.

44. Hegyi A. Region-dependent hamstrings activity in Nordic hamstring exercise and stiff-leg deadlift defined with high-density electromyography. *Scand J Med Sci Sports*, 2018. 28: 992.

45. Bridgeman LA. Relationships between concentric and eccentric strength and countermovement jump performance in resistance trained men. *J Strength Cond Res*, 2018. 32: 255.

46. Coratella G. Specific adaptations in performance and muscle architecture after weighted jump-squat vs. body mass squat jump training in recreational soccer players. *J Strength Cond Res*, 2018. 32: 921.

47. Alonso-Fernandez D. Changes in muscle architecture of biceps femoris induced by eccentric strength training with Nordic hamstring exercise. *Scand J Med Sci Sports*, 2018. 28: 88.

48. Alt T. Velocity-specific and time-dependent adaptations following a standardized Nordic hamstring exercise training. *Scand J Med Sci Sports*, 2018. 28: 65.

49. Coratella G. Greater fatigability in knee-flexors vs. knee-extensors after a standardized fatiguing protocol. *Eur J Sport Sci*, 2018.

50. Coratella G. Running fatiguing protocol affects peak torque joint angle and peak torque differently in hamstrings vs. quadriceps. *Sport Sci Health*, 2018. 14: 193.

TEAM BALL SPORTS

HIP WORK

1. Morcelli MH. Hip muscles strength and activation in older fallers and non-fallers. *Am J Sports Med*, 2015. 43: 1316.

CLASSIC HIP PROBLEMS

2. Orchard JW. Men at higher risk of groin injuries in elite team sports: a systematic review. *Br J Sports Med*, 2015. 49: 798.

3. Audenaert EA. Hip morphological characteristics and range of internal rotation in femoroacetabular impingement. *Am J Sports Med*, 2012. 40: 1329.

4. Hafiz E. Do anatomical or other hip characteristics predispose to lower limb musculoskeletal injury? A systematic review. *Med Sci Sports Exerc*, 2013. 45 (suppl. 1): S5.

5. Hanney W. Body weight adjusted hip strength ratios in the weight training population. *J Strength Cond Res*, 2014. 28: 71.

6. Kemp JL. Greater understanding of normal hip physical function may guide clinicians in providing targeted rehabilitation programs. *J Sci Med Sport*, 2013. 16: 292.

7. Mosler AB. Which factors differentiate athletes with hip/groin pain from those without? A systematic review with meta-analysis. *Br J Sports Med*, 2015. 49: 810.

8. Jensen J. Eccentric strengthening effect of hip-adductor training with resistance bands in soccer players: a randomised controlled trial. *Br J Sports Med*, 2014. 48: 332.

9. Whittaker JL. Risk factors for groin injury in sport: an updated systematic review. *Br J Sports Med*, 2015. 49: 803.

10. Hrysomallis C. Hip adductors' strength, flexibility, and injury risk. *J Strength Cond Res*, 2009. 23: 1514.

11. Piva SR. Strength around the hip and flexibility of soft tissues in individuals with and without patellofemoral pain syndrome. *J Orthop Sports Phys Ther*, 2005. 35: 793.

12. Jeon HJ. Effectiveness of hip abductor strengthening on patellofemoral pain syndrome patients: a meta-analysis. *J Athl Train*, 2014. 49 (suppl.): S203.

13. Dolak KL. Hip strengthening prior to functional exercises reduces pain sooner than quadriceps strengthening in females with patellofemoral pain syndrome: a randomized clinical trial. *J Orthop Sports Phys Ther*, 2011. 41: 560.

14. DeJong A. Ultrasound imaging reveals gluteal muscle changes during gait in healthy individuals with medial knee displacement. *J Athl Train*, 2018. 53 (suppl.): S258.

15. Stearns KM. Improvements in hip muscle performance result in increased use of the hip extensors and abductors during a landing task. *Am J Sports Med*, 2014. 42: 602.

16. Powers CM. Hip strength as a predictor of ankle sprains in male soccer players: a prospective study. *J Athl Train*, 2017. 52: 1048.

17. Dix J. The relationship between hip muscle strength and dynamic knee valgus in asymptomatic females: a systematic review. *Phys Ther Sport*, 2018.

18. Noriega-Guerra A. Muscle chains stretching effect for chronic pubalgia in athletes. *J Athl Train*, 2017. 52: 874.

19. Dupre T. Does inside passing contribute to the high incidence of groin injuries in soccer? A biomechanical analysis. *J Sports Sci*, 2018. 36.

20. Evans KL. Reduced severity of lumbopelvic-hip injuries in professional Rugby Union players following tailored preventative programmes. *J Sports Sci Med*, 2018. 21: 274.

21. Larruskain J. A comparison of injuries in elite male and female football players: a five season prospective study. *Scand J Med Sci Sports*, 2017.

HOW DO THE HAMSTRINGS PROTECT THE CRUCIATE LIGAMENTS?

22. Solomonow M. The synergistic action of the anterior cruciate ligament and thigh muscles in maintaining joint stability. *Am J Sports Med*, 1987. 15: 207.

GOLF AND SPORTS INVOLVING ROTATION

1. Walsh BA. Golf-related injuries treated in United States emergency departments. *Am J Emerg Med*, 2017. 35: 1666.

BACK PAIN: THE GOLFER'S PARADOX

2. Harrison K. Low back pain in recreational golfers. *J Athl Train*, 2018. 53 (suppl.): S355.

IMPROVE ABDOMINAL AND LUMBAR SUPPORT

3. Vleeming A. The functional coupling of the deep abdominal and paraspinal muscles: the effects of simulated paraspinal muscle contraction on force transfer to the middle and posterior layer of the thoracolumbar fascia. *J Anat*, 2014. 225.

4. Martuscello JM. Systematic review of core muscle activity during physical fitness exercises. *J Strength Cond Res*, 2013. 27: 1684.

HOW TO STABILIZE THE SHOULDERS EFFECTIVELY

5. Lee CH. Features of golf-related shoulder pain in Korean amateur golfers. *Ann Rehabil Med*, 2017. 41: 394.

SWIMMING AND NAUTICAL SPORTS

MUSCLES USED IN SWIMMING

1. Antonio J. Bone mineral density in competitive athletes. *J Exerc Nutr*, 2018. 1.

UNDERSTANDING SHOULDER PAIN IN ATHLETES

2. Timmons MK. Fatigue of the lower trapezius produces decreased acromial humeral distance. *J Athl Train*, 2018. 53 (suppl.): S185.

3. Gaudet S. Evolution of muscular fatigue in periscapular and rotator cuff muscles during isokinetic shoulder rotations. *J Sports Sci*, 2018. 36.

STRENGTH TRAINING TO OVERCOME SHOULDER PAIN

4. Paulson G. The effects of a shoulder strengthening program on scapular positioning in collegiate swimmers. *J Athl Train*, 2018. 53 (suppl.): S180.

RACQUET AND THROWING SPORTS

ELBOW PAIN AND TENNIS ELBOW

1. Pexa BS. The effects of loading parameters and elbow flexion angle on medial elbow joint space. *J Athl Train*, 2018. 53 (suppl.): S182.

CYCLING AND ROAD SPORTS

THE EFFECTS OF STRENGTH TRAINING ON A CYCLIST'S ENDURANCE

1. Sunde A. Maximal strength training improves cycling economy in competitive cyclists. *J Strength Cond Res*, 2010. 24: 2157.
2. Yamamoto LM. The effects of resistance training on road cycling performance among highly trained cyclists: a systematic review. *J Strength Cond Res*, 2010. 24: 560.
3. Trevino M. The effects of 10 weeks of continuous cycling on maximal aerobic capacity and motor unit behavior of the vastus lateralis. *J Strength Cond Res*, 2017. 31 (suppl. 1): S2.
4. Sterczala A. The effects of eight weeks of resistance training on motor unit behavior of the vastus lateralis. *J Strength Cond Res*, 2017. 31 (suppl. 1): S3.

SPECIFIC INJURIES

5. Bini RR. Potential factors associated with knee pain in cyclists: a systematic review. *Open Access J Sports Med*, 2018. 9: 99.
6. Sabo D. Bone quality in the lumbar spine in high-performance athletes. *Eur Spine J*, 1996. 5: 258.
7. Mathis SL. Resistance training is associated with higher lumbar spine and hip bone mineral density in competitive male cyclists. *J Strength Cond Res*, 2018. 32: 274.

COMBAT SPORTS

1. Delavier F, Gundill M. *Musculation pour le fight et les sports de combat*, Editions Vigot, 2012.

STRATEGIES TO PREVENT INJURIES

2. Del Vecchio FB. Blessures dans les arts martiaux et les sports de combat: prevalence, caracteristiques et mecanismes. *Sci Sports*, 2018. 33: 158.
3. Cimen Polat S. Analysis of the relationship between elite wrestlers' leg strength and balance performance, and injury history. *Sports*, 2018. 6: 35.

PART II

EXERCISES FOR RUNNING SPORTS

GLUTE-HAM RAISE (GHR), RAZOR CURL, AND NORDIC HAMSTRING CURL

1. Oliver GD. Comparison of hamstring and gluteus muscles electromyographic activity while performing the razor curl vs. the traditional prone hamstring curl. *J Strength Cond Res*, 2009. 23: 2250.

STANDING CALF RAISE

2. Mock S. Correlation of dynamic strength in the standing calf raise with sprinting performance in consecutive sections up to 30 meters. *Res Sports Med*, 2018.
3. Geremia JM. Effects of high loading by eccentric triceps surae training on Achilles tendon properties in humans. *Eur J Appl Physiol*, 2018. 118: 1725.
4. Lee SSM. Built for speed: musculoskeletal structure and sprinting ability. *J Exp Biol*, 2009. 212: 3700.
5. Nedimyer AK. Foot intrinsic muscle function and activation, and exercise related leg pain in runners. *J Athl Train*, 2018. 53 (suppl.): S149.

TOWEL CURL

6. Takashi S. Effect of the towel curl exercise on the medial longitudinal arch of the foot. *Phys Ther Sport*, 2017. 28: e15.

EXERCISES FOR TEAM BALL SPORTS

1. Katis A. Bilateral leg differences in soccer kick kinematics following exhaustive running fatigue. *Asian J Sports Med*, 2017. 8: e33680.

EXERCISES FOR GOLF AND SPORTS INVOLVING ROTATION

PLANK

1. Whyte EF. Effects of a dynamic core stability program on the biomechanics of cutting maneuvers: a randomized controlled trial. *Scand J Med Sci Sports*, 2017.
2. Gonzalez SL. Risk factors of low back pain in female collegiate rowers. *J Athl Train*, 2017. 52 (suppl.): S31.
3. Raabe ME. Biomechanical consequences of running with deep core muscle weakness. *J Biomech*, 2018.
4. Lipinski CL. Surface electromyography of the forearm musculature during an overhead throwing rehabilitation progression program. *Phys Ther Sport*, 2018.
5. Aboodarda SJ. Pain pressure threshold of a muscle tender spot increases following local and non-local rolling massage. *BMC Musculoskelet Disord*, 2015. 16: 265.
6. Cavanaugh MT. An acute session of roller massage prolongs voluntary torque development and diminishes evoked pain. *Eur J Appl Physiol*, 2017. 117: 109.

EXERCISES FOR COMBAT SPORTS

BRIDGE (HIP THRUST)

1. Fimland AV. Electromyographic comparison of barbell deadlift, hex bar deadlift and hip thrust exercises: a cross-over study. *J Strength Cond Res*, 2017.

SQUAT WITH A TRAP BAR OR ON A DEADLIFT MACHINE

2. Choe K. Comparing the back squat and deadlift. *J Strength Cond Res*, 2017. 31 (suppl. 1): S13.
3. Snyder B. Comparison of muscle activity during the Olympic deadlift and a walk-in deadlift machine. *J Strength Cond Res*, 2014. 28.
4. Swinton PA. A biomechanical analysis of straight and hexagonal barbell deadlifts using submaximal loads. *J Strength Cond Res*, 2011. 25: 2000.

PART III

PREPARING TO WORK OUT

1. Serra R. The influence weekly resistance training frequency on strength and body composition. *Int J Sports Sci*, 2018. 8: 19.
2. Moran-Navarro R. Time course of recovery following resistance training leading or not to failure. *Eur J Appl Physiol*, 2017. 117: 2387.

WARM-UP PROGRAMS TO DO BEFORE STRENGTH TRAINING OR BEFORE PLAYING YOUR SPORT

3. Nickerson B. Effect of cluster set warm-up configurations on sprint performance in collegiate male soccer players. *Physiol Appl Nutr Métab*, 2018.
4. Dello Iacono A. Loaded hip thrust-based PAP protocol effects on acceleration and sprint performance of handball players. *J Sports Sci*, 2018.

PROGRAMS TO BRING A SPECIFIC WEAK AREA UP TO PAR

5. Colston MA. Lumbar multifidus cross sectional area as a possible predictor of injury among college football players. *J Athl Train*, 2018. 53 (suppl.): S103.
6. Mason J. Ipsilateral corticomotor responses are confined to the homologous muscle following cross-education of muscular strength. *Physiol Appl Nutr Métab*, 2018. 43: 11.

7. Del Bel MJ. A hierarchy in functional muscle roles at the knee is influenced by sex and anterior cruciate ligament deficiency. *Clin Biochem*, 2018. 57: 129.

8. Omi Y. Effect of hip-focused injury prevention training for anterior cruciate ligament injury reduction in female basketball players: a 12-year prospective intervention study. *Am J Sports Med*, 2018. 46: 852.

9. Smith BI. Effects of hip strengthening on neuromuscular control, hip strength, and self-reported functional deficits in individuals with chronic ankle instability. *J Sport Rehab*, 2018. 27.

10. Lee JWY. Eccentric hamstring strength deficit and poor hamstring-to-quadriceps ratio are risk factors for hamstring strain injury in football: a prospective study of 146 professional players. *J Sports Sci Med*, 2018. 21.

11. Lantto I. Epidemiology of Achilles tendon ruptures: increasing incidence over a 33-year period. *Scand J Med Sci Sports*, 2015. 25: e133.

TRAINING PROGRAMS FOR VARIOUS SPORTS

12. Mole JL. The effect of transversus abdominis activation on exercise-related transient abdominal pain. *J Sci Med Sport*, 2014. 17: 261.

13. Collins J. Football nutrition: time for a new consensus. *BJSM*, 2017. 51: 1577.

14. Inacio Salles J. Effect of specific exercise strategy on strength and proprioception in volleyball players with infraspinatus muscle atrophy. *Scand J Med Sci Sports*, 2018.

15. Sheehan WB. Examination of the neuromechanical factors contributing to golf swing performance. *J Sports Sci*, 2018.

16. Grover KJ. Prevalence of shoulder pain in competitive archery. *Asian J Sports Med*, 2017. 8: e40971.

17. Kojima T. Lumbar intervertebral disc degeneration in professional surfers. *Sports Orthop Traumatol*, 2018.

18. Furness J. Profiling shoulder strength in competitive surfers. *Sports*, 2018. 6: 52.

19. Lamborn LC. Trunk performance in players with superior and poor serve mechanics. *J Athl Train*, 2016. 51 (suppl.): S80.

20. Gescheit DT. A multi-year injury epidemiology analysis of an elite national junior tennis program. *J Sports Sci Med*, 2018.

21. Nodehi-Moghadam A. A comparative study on shoulder rotational strength, range of motion and proprioception between the throwing athletes and non-athletic persons. *Asian J Sports Med*, 2013. 4: 34.

22. Pellegrini B. CrossÐcountry skiing movement factorization to explore relationships between skiing economy and athletes' skills. *Scand J Med Sci Sports*, 2017.

POST-TRAINING RECOVERY PROGRAMS

23. Fukano M. Foot posture alteration and recovery following a full marathon run. *Eur J Sport Science*, 2018.

24. Souza-Silva E. Blood flow after contraction and cuff occlusion is reduced in subjects with muscle soreness after eccentric exercise. *Scand J Med Sci in Sports*, 2018.

WARNING

This publication is written and published to provide accurate and authoritative information relevant to the subject matter presented. It is published and sold with the understanding that the author and publisher are not engaged in rendering legal, medical, or other professional services by reason of their authorship or publication of this work. If medical or other expert assistance is required, the services of a competent professional person should be sought.

ACKNOWLEDGMENTS
Thanks to our models, Yann, Djalil, Axel Sousa Pintori, and Maxime Miquel, who were all readers of our previous books.

Yann   Djalil   Axel Sousa Pintori   Maxime Miquel

Library of Congress Cataloging-in-Publication Data

Names: Delavier, Frédéric, author. | Gundill, Michael, author.
Title: Strength training anatomy for athletes / Frédéric Delavier,
  Michael Gundill.
Other titles: Guide de musculation pour les sportifs. English.
Description: Champaign, IL : Human Kinetics, 2019 | "This book is a
  revised edition of Guide de musculation pour les sportifs, published in
  2019 by Éditions Vigot." | Includes bibliographical references and
  index.
Identifiers: LCCN 2019049914 | ISBN 9781492597414 (paperback)
Subjects: LCSH: Muscles--Anatomy. | Weight training. | Muscle strength.
Classification: LCC QM151 .D45313 2020 | DDC 611/.73--dc23
LC record available at https://lccn.loc.gov/2019049914

ISBN: 978-1-4925-9741-4 (print)

Copyright © 2019 by Éditions Vigot, 23 rue de l'École de Médecine, 75006 Paris, France

Human Kinetics supports copyright. Copyright fuels scientific and artistic endeavor, encourages authors to create new works, and promotes free speech. Thank you for buying an authorized edition of this work and for complying with copyright laws by not reproducing, scanning, or distributing any part of it in any form without written permission from the publisher. You are supporting authors and allowing Human Kinetics to continue to publish works that increase the knowledge, enhance the performance, and improve the lives of people all over the world.

This book is a revised edition of *Guide de Musculation Pour les Sportifs,* published in 2019 by Éditions Vigot.

Photography: © Michael Gundill; **Illustrations:** © Frédéric Delavier; **Production:** Patrick Leleux PAO; **Photoengraving:** IGS-CP

Printed in France   10 9 8 7 6 5 4 3 2 1

Human Kinetics
1607 North Market Street
Champaign, IL 61820
Website: www.HumanKinetics.com